Excuse Me!

Excuse Me!

OUTRAGEOUS PLAYS FOR SECONDARY STUDENTS

Hazel Edwards

Copyright © Hazel Edwards 2025

All rights reserved. No part of this book may be reproduced or transmitted in any form or by any means, electronic or mechanical, including photocopying, recording or by any information storage and retrieval system, without prior permission in writing from the publisher.

First published in 1998 by Pearson Education
This edition published in 2025 by Amba Press, Melbourne, Australia

www.ambapress.com.au

Cover design: Tess McCabe
Internal design: Amba Press
Proofreader: Sarah Fallon

ISBN: 9781923215580 (pbk)
ISBN: 9781923215597 (ebk)

A catalogue record for this book is available from the National Library of Australia.

Contents

About the author	vii
Introduction	1
Using Playscripts	3
The Not-So-Great Excuse Machine	7
Everyperson	33
The Fairly Fake TV Show	45
The Mt Paperwork Whodunnit	73
The Minutes of Time	91

About the author

Hazel Edwards, OAM, is an award-winning author of books for children, teachers and adults. Writing and teaching are creative 'ideas' occupations and in recent years Hazel has been scripting in new mediums for class performance, puppetry, screen and theatre. She has also initiated translations and dual language stories.

Initially, this passion for writing continued alongside working in a secondary school and lecturing at teachers' college. Aged twenty-seven, Hazel published her first novel, *General Store*, a book based on life in a rural town, now re-issued as part of the University of Melbourne, UnTapped Project of historic Australian literature.

Her children's picture book classic, *There's a Hippopotamus on Our Roof Eating Cake* (1980) has been cherished by children and parents alike and led to the dubious honour of Hazel being referred to as 'the Hippo Lady'. The ageless *There's a Hippopotamus on Our Roof Eating Cake* has been reprinted annually, evolved into a series of seven picture books and inspired a junior chapter book, classroom playscripts, a musical stage production and a short movie. Translations exist in Mandarin, Braille and Auslan signing for the hearing impaired.

Alongside creating quirky, feisty characters in her easy-to-read junior chapter books, Hazel writes adult mysteries and has published over 220 books across a range of 'social issues', fun subjects and genres. Published titles include *f2m:the boy within*, the first co-written by a transman, a YA novel about gender transition, and now being drawn as a graphic novel by Ryan Kennedy and another transman. Her YA #Clific novel *Wasted?*, features innovative asylum seekers trading bio-fuel for visas from their new mid ocean state around the Great Garbage Patches, from the viewpoint of a teen refugee Kit who draws solutions.

Hazel has collaborated with experts to publish adult non-fiction titles such as *Difficult Personalities* (translated into seven languages). She mentors 'Hazelnuts' to craft interesting memoirs and family histories in her workshops based on her 'Writing a Non-Boring Family History'. Recently a 'Complete Your Book in a Year' course has been offered via Zoom. Awarded the Australian Antarctic Division Arts Fellowship (2001), Hazel travelled to Casey Station on the 'Polar Bird' ice-ship. This visit inspired a range of creative projects including the young adult eco-thriller *Antarctica's Frozen Chosen*, picture book *Antarctic Dad* as well as classroom playscripts.

Hazel has been a guest writer-in-residence in communities across Australia, a visiting author to Pasir Ridge International School in Indonesia and an author ambassador to Youfu West Street International School in Nanjing, China.

Passionate about literacy and creativity, Hazel has mentored gifted students and held the title of Reading Ambassador for various organisations. Formerly a director on the Committee of Management of the Australian Society of Authors, Hazel was awarded an OAM for Literature in 2013. She is the patron of the Society of Women Writers (Vic) and in 2022 she was awarded the Monash University Distinguished Alumni Award for Education. She writes a birthday story such as 'Go! Go! Gecko' as a gift of the imagination for each grandson.

Introduction

Initially, I set out to make the themes in the following plays as topical and relevant as possible. A play about 'managing technological change', another about 'making crucial choices within the casino of life', 'a satirical look at the media', plus a 'Mt Paperwork Whodunnit' which is versatile for local adaptation and a 'futuristic look at time as currency'.

The other aim was to make the plays accessible within the limits of a classroom. Each play's performance fits within a forty-minute period, though *The Mt Paperwork Whodunnit* can take longer and be made more complex. Simple settings and props are easily found or made, and casting can involve ten to twenty-five actors. The speeches are varied enough in length to allow for differing students' abilities. As well as roles for proficient readers, there are a number of non-speaking parts and choruses, SFX technicians, and so on.

Another objective was to present content which would lead to thoughtful class discussion. This is most obvious in *Everyperson*, where the cast and audience must seek their own resolution and ending. In between, my intention is for students and teachers to have fun. I hope you do.

Using Playscripts

Playscripts offer opportunities for educators and schools to make learning fun and relevant. Including performances in the curriculum offers benefits beyond traditional literary study, touching on social development, creativity, and academic achievement.

Enhancing literacy and language skills

Playscripts provide students with literature that integrates:

- Dialogue-based reading that improves fluency and expression
- Rich vocabulary in context of natural conversations
- Multiple perspectives and voices
- Comprehension of character motivations

Building social and emotional skills

Through working with playscripts, students develop:

- Empathy by stepping into different characters' perspectives
- Collaboration skills through group reading and performance

- Confidence through public speaking opportunities
- Emotional intelligence through character analysis and portrayal

Cross-curricular applications

Playscripts enhance learning across subjects:

- Social Studies: Exploring cultural perspectives and social issues
- Language Arts: Strengthening writing and analytical skills
- Arts Education: Integrating performance, design and creative expression

Active learning benefits

The interactive nature of playscripts promotes:

- Physical engagement through movement and gesture
- Vocal expression and speech development
- Memory enhancement through role learning
- Critical thinking through character interpretation

Accessibility and differentiation

Playscripts support diverse learners by offering:

- Multiple reading levels within a single text
- Visual and kinaesthetic learning opportunities
- Collaborative learning environments
- Varied and non-speaking roles that accommodate different ability levels

Assessment opportunities

Some assessment opportunities could include:

- Performance-based evaluation
- Writing original scenes or adaptations
- Character analysis assignments
- Collaborative project work

Cultural and community benefits

Using playscripts can:

- Build school community through shared creative experiences
- Create connections with local theatre organisations
- Provide opportunities for family involvement
- Celebrate diverse cultural perspectives

The Not-So-Great Excuse Machine

A classroom play for secondary students

A playscript of approximately 40 minutes performance time

Rationale

This play explores the crucial theme of managing change in the workplace, a particularly relevant topic for students on the cusp of entering their professional lives. While young people typically embrace new technology with ease, they often encounter workplace environments where colleagues remain attached to outdated, labour-intensive methods simply because they're familiar. Through the accessible and humorous lens of 'excuses', the play examines how resistance to high-tech innovations can significantly impact workplace productivity.

By approaching this serious management concept through comedy, students are encouraged to engage in deeper discussions about the economic and social implications of technological change, moving beyond mere surface-level entertainment to understand the real-world challenges of workplace transformation.

Outline

The Excuse Emporium provides excuses for those in need. However, the Excuse Bin isn't handling all the work and more help is needed.

The situation changes when the inventor of a hi-tech Automatic Excuse Machine (AEM), which offers degrees of excuses ranging from ordinary to super deluxe, gives the Excuse Emporium a free trial.

Cast

Several parts can be played by any gender.

For a small cast of actors, some parts can be taken by one person, such as Sasha/Toni, Miles/Chris, Queue, Excuses.

Minimum cast number: 10

Maximum cast number: 25 plus

- BOSS: Harassed small-business person. Prepared to use any opportunity to improve the business.
- ASSISTANT: Young and quick-witted.
- LATE-HARRI: Employee who is always late. Should look permanently hassled.
- WORRIER: Carries bags labelled 'worries'.
- SASHA: Wears No-Error-Wash uniform. Carries laundry.
- TONI: Fruit seller with sack of apples labelled 'Best Fruit in Town'.
- MILES: Student with computer problem.
- CHRIS: Romantic boy. Carries very large St Valentine's Day card.
- QUEUE: Any number. Can be students, workers, pets, neighbours.
- EXCUSES: Any number. They appear all together in a bin.
- SECURITY SHREDDER: Wears overalls and carries a spanner. One leg in plaster.
- UNION ORGANISER: Carries placard labelled 'Join Your Union Here' and recorder.

- INVENTOR: Crazy professor and computer nerd. This is the most demanding role.
- AEM: This role is a voice only: mechanical, robotic sounding.

Technicians

- Creator of sound effects (SFX)
- Props co-ordinator: person responsible for building or collecting suitable props

Sound effects (SFX)

- Phone ringing
- Phone voices
- Machine noises

Props

- Box for Excuses (large enough for people to fit inside)
- Excuses signs, such as 'best excuses in town'
- Envelope marked 'late excuse'
- Bags of worries (labelled with individual worries)
- Mobile phone
- Recorder
- Union placard 'Join your Union Here'
- Automatic Excuse Machine or AEM (large enough for one person to hide inside and able to break apart at the end)
- Rolls of toilet paper
- Laundry basket of odd socks
- Sack of apples
- Computer discs/USBs
- Oversized St Valentine's Day card
- Dictionary

Setting

- Office space and counter
- Signs reading:
    - BEST EXCUSES IN TOWN
    - SHOP FOR ALL EXCUSES HERE
    - PURCHASE NOW, EXCUSE YOURSELF LATER
    - TRY OUR BARGAIN PARDONS
    - PERUSE OUR EXCUSE
- In front of the stage there should be a very large cardboard box where the Excuses sit

Script

LATE-HARRI: *[races in]* Sorry I'm late.

BOSS: *[consults watch]* What's your excuse? No excuse and you lose your pay.

LATE-HARRI: That's the trouble. I can't think of one.

BOSS: Not good enough. Around here we stock and sell excuses.

LATE-HARRI: But I told you before, I can't think of one.

BOSS: Have a look in the bin.

[Late-Harri dips into the Excuses Bin.]

[SFX-phone rings]

BOSS: How come I always have to answer the phone? *[picks up phone]* Hello. Excuses Emporium here.

[SFX-loud phone voice noises]

BOSS: Yes. We offer excuses at bargain rates. Our prices are the lowest in town. *[hangs up. To Late-Harri]* Well, have you found one yet?

LATE-HARRI: *[upside down in bin]* Not yet.

[Excuse No 1 holds out envelope marked LATE EXCUSE.]

LATE-HARRI: My alarm didn't work.

BOSS: *[impatiently]* Can't you do better than that?

[Late-Harri pulls out another. This time Excuse No 2 holds up placard.]

The Not-So-Great Excuse Machine

EXCUSE 2:	Somebody stole half my bike.
BOSS:	Which half?
EXCUSE 2:	The wheels.
LATE-HARRI:	Fantastic. Only I haven't got a bike. *[burrows back in bin. Brings out Excuse No 3.]*
EXCUSE 3:	Well, it's like this. I woke in the middle of the night. A green light was hovering over my bed. It trapped me so I couldn't move. Then I heard a voice saying, 'You have been chosen to represent all humanity in the Intergalactic Games.' Next thing, I was zapped into the Galaxy I took part in the Marathon. The Marathon took a million light years. So that's why I'm late.
LATE-HARRI:	Was it a UFO?
EXCUSE 2:	Yes. A UFO. It was an Utterly Fabulous Opportunity...
BOSS:	*[interrupting]* Hey, didn't we use that Excuse last week? What's wrong with your filing system? Time you Excuses started to work more efficiently
WORRIER:	*[jumping the queue and dumping bags of worries on counter]* My name is Worrier, spelt W.O.R.R.I.E.R.
QUEUE:	*[vigorously interjecting]* Hey, we were here first. What do you think you're doing? Some people will try anything. Get back into line.
WORRIER:	*[ignoring Queue]* I want to buy a few Excuses in advance.

ASSISTANT: *[rather bossy tone]* Well, you're out of luck. We're running a bit short. Our Excuses Bin isn't keeping up with the demand. Some of our Excuses are wearing thin, and some are out of date. You'd better come back next week.

WORRIER: But bad things might happen soon. I might make a mistake. I want to be ready with an excuse, just in case.

QUEUE: *[together]* Jumping the queue was your mistake.

WORRIER: *[to Queue]* Excuse me. So I need another excuse already?

LATE-HARRI: We're running out of good excuses. Our people are taking too long to think of new ones.

BOSS: Maybe we need some new ideas? Maybe the old ones need early retirement. I know, I know … *[picks up mobile phone]* I'll ring around and see what I can find. *[heads for wings talking into phone]*

QUEUE: *[pressing around counter and all talking at once]* How about some service?
I need an excuse for getting home late.
Blowing up the microwave, almost!
Barking all night.
Emptying the school swimming pool an hour before the carnival.
Putting glue in the hamburger mix. Breaking my diet … again.
Not having a partner for the school dance.
Writing off the car on my first lesson.
Not being able to spell excuse, or is it X-CUSE?

[Boss returns to counter and tries to pacify Queue. Inventor enters pushing Automatic Excuses Machine.]

INVENTOR: How do you do? I hear you are running a little low on stock. Could I introduce you to my Automatic Excuse Machine? No excuse disputed. No excuse challenged. Our excuses are guaranteed. Would you like a week's trial?

BOSS: *[suspiciously]* How much is it going to cost?

INVENTOR: *[indignantly]* Did I say anything about cost? I'll have you know this is a week's free trial. No deposit. Send it back if you don't like it. This is an opportunity your firm can't afford to miss.

BOSS: Okay, okay. *[examines AEM very carefully]*

ASSISTANT: Can't think of an excuse for not using it.

[Everyone gathers around machine. Excuses protest from inside their bin. Union Organiser enters waving placard and carrying a recorder.]

WORRIER: Is there an Excuses Union? That's a worry.

UNION ORGANISER: *[to Boss]* If you automate without negotiating with the Union, this Excuses Bin will go on strike.

BOSS: Let them. They're hopeless. Time we downsized. Time we became more efficient.

UNION ORGANISER: Our workers are giving their best. If you demand more, the quality of their service will suffer. Do you want a situation where there's a 'go slow' or a 'work-to-rules', or the plant is closed down? No. Sticking to quality is the only way.

BOSS: What quality? All I get is the same excuses.

UNION ORGANISER: Industrial relations is a highly specialised area. Special expertise is needed for negotiating for anything above the award. What are your qualifications?

BOSS: Qualifications! What are you talking about? Don't I own the premises and the business? Don't I allow your people to have their union fees deducted from their weekly wages at my expense?

UNION ORGANISER: Yes, well ... that has been the custom for a long time.

ASSISTANT: For as long as I can remember.

BOSS: See? It's time for a change. New technology means bigger profits, and isn't this what we all want?

[Excuses climb out of bin protesting.]

UNION ORGANISER: *[holds out recorder]* Record your complaints, record your complaints.

EXCUSES: *[firing in turn]*
But they've always used us.
We've always done things this way. You can't trust a machine.
A machine can't think like us. They always break down.
What if the power goes off?
We're cheaper.
And we're much more experienced.

INVENTOR: *[ignoring protests]* Let me give you a demonstration of how the AEM, the Automatic Excuse Machine, works.

[in a humorous way, the Inventor demonstrates the hi-tech efficiency of the AEM]

BOSS: The most frequent request is for a homework excuse. What do you offer?

[Inventor works on the keyboard]

[SFX-of machine working very hard]

INVENTOR: My excuses menu offers fifty-seven different categories for incomplete, late, mislaid or misunderstood homework. We even have a category for those who can't spell, and another for cheats-with penalties of course. For example, a week's late assignment with messy writing can buy the ordinary, the giant size, or the super deluxe model.

ASSISTANT: That's the sales pitch. Now how about a real excuse?

[toilet roll streams out of machine]

AEM: *[uses funny machine voice]* The dog threw up over my homework and you wouldn't want to smell it.

EXCUSES: Not bad.
Heard it before.
How about something new?

INVENTOR: That's only an ordinary excuse. The giant-sized excuse is ... *[presses more buttons]*

AEM: Our house burnt down. Luckily, my homework was left with the next door neighbour. Unluckily, the paper was used to clean up the fire damage. And the back of one sheet was used to write the fire insurance claim.

BOSS:	Not bad.
EXCUSES:	*[terribly upset and all together]* Almost good. Too good. No wonder they are trying to replace us with technology. Now we'll get the sack for sure. What'll we do?
ASSISTANT:	*[ignores Excuses and speaks to Boss]* What do you mean, not bad. That was terrific.
LATE-HARRI:	I'm still not convinced. Can't that machine do any better?
INVENTOR:	Well, if those two excuses don't work for you, try our super deluxe model. *[works on machine]*
AEM:	A hacker lifted my maths homework to insert into the NASA space program. It was used to launch the X-rocket which is currently circling Mars. It's due back in our orbit on 29th February 2027.
LATE-HARRI:	But 2027 isn't a leap year.
WORRIER:	So it'll never come back.
QUEUE:	Don't worry about that. You'll never have to do your homework. What a terrific excuse.
EXCUSES BIN:	*[together]* It's the perfect excuse … unfortunately … *[much moaning and groaning. They disappear inside the box.]*
INVENTOR:	*[beaming]* Exactly.
BOSS:	What an excellent demo. I'm impressed. You've convinced me. We'll buy this new technology

	to update the business. And now I'll arrange for the Security Shredder to downsize the Excuses Bin. That way we'll save on wages, tax, sick pay, holiday pay, insurance, long service and parental leave.
EXCUSES:	*[pop up out of box, horrified]* We're going to be shredded?
BOSS:	See it more as recycling.
ASSISTANT:	*[fed up with the Excuses Bin always whinging]* Yes, recycled as garden mulch.
EXCUSES:	*[frantic whispering to Union Organiser]* Find a life saving excuse. Quickly.
UNION ORGANISER:	*[flustered]* You … we … need an excuse to justify our existence. An excuse for being … here.
SECURITY SHREDDER:	*[limps in]* Sorry I'm late. Which ones do you want shredded, boss? *[heads for Excuses Bin]*
UNION ORGANISER:	*[in a panic to Bin]* Quick, some excuses for being late.
EXCUSES BIN:	*[wildly, in turn]* He was just leaving on time when the cat tripped him. And he fell over. And broke his leg. So they took him to hospital. And they took ages. To put on the plaster.
LATE-HARRI:	*[scornfully]* Who'd believe that?
SECURITY SHREDDER:	*[surprised]* I would. That's what actually happened.

ASSISTANT:	Maybe. But it's not a great excuse. Maybe if you'd said, 'I tripped over the size-ten foot of a giant crocodile which just happened to be nibbling my toes'.
	Or 'I ran into a purple rhino who sat on my car squashing it so I couldn't get here on time'.
	Or 'an alien just happened to come past in his flying saucer. He flew me to Mars and zapped into my brain so that when I was returned I couldn't remember where I was supposed to be ...' then we might agree that you've got a great excuse.
SECURITY SHREDDER:	Those excuses are just too childish. Anyway, it wasn't like that.
BOSS:	So how was it?
SECURITY SHREDDER:	I told you before. Now I'll just shift these Excuses out of everybody's way. *[starts to move Excuses Bin from centre of stage]*
SASHA:	*[enters wearing a 'No-Error-Wash' uniform. Dumps basket of laundry on counter]* Thirty-nine socks. And none of them match. Does anyone belong to these? *[Sasha checks Queues legs for socks]*
QUEUE:	Hey, what do you think you're doing? Leave my feet alone. Can't you see I'm wearing sandals? Stop tickling my toes.
SASHA:	This is the sock exchange, isn't it?
ASSISTANT:	No. We only trade in excuses.
SASHA:	Excuses for lost socks?
ASSISTANT:	*[frowning]* Haven't been asked for them before.

WORRIER:	I'm always losing my socks.
UNION ORGANISER:	Now there's an idea. *[confers with Excuses]*
INVENTOR:	*[taps Sasha on the shoulder]* I think my invention can fix your problem.
SASHA:	What is your invention?
INVENTOR:	The Automatic Excuse Machine. It works like this: My machine is programmed to present an excuse for any possible problem. All you have to do is feed it in, and wait for the machine to come up with an answer.
SASHA:	Really? Your machine interests me. What are the best excuses for losing one sock?
	[Inventor feeds problem into machine] *[SFX-machine working]*
AEM:	We make these suggestions: Tell the owners that you lost their socks on purpose. You see, those who only wear one sock are artistic. If they won't accept that excuse, tell them that red and green colour-blind people don't mind wearing odd socks. Neither do absent-minded customers. Our final suggestion is that you start a new fashion.
EXCUSES BIN:	*[puzzled]* They're not excuses, they're just reasons for wearing odd socks.
ASSISTANT:	Right. Some people don't know the difference between excuses, reasons and solutions.
SASHA:	But I don't need excuses if I've got solutions.
ASSISTANT:	*[searches through dictionary]* It says here in the dictionary, 'Excuse: a pardon, overlook a slight offence, be a justification of a fault or error:

	release of an obligation.' It also says a reason put forward for excusing a fault.
WORRIER:	I don't understand all that. So what's the difference between a reason and an excuse?
LATE-HARRI:	Probably the time you give the excuse. Like I'm always too late for things. I wonder if you can give an excuse beforehand for being late?
WORRIER:	Then it becomes a reason. Let's say you invite me to come to your house, only I've already agreed to go rollerblading with Fred. So Fred is my reason for not coming.
ASSISTANT:	What if you didn't want to go anyway?
BOSS:	Then that's a white lie.
UNION ORGANISER:	*[officiously]* Sounds racist to me. We'd be pretty quick to blackban that.
SASHA:	*[becoming impatient with conversation. To Inventor]* I'll buy all of those excuses. *[proceeds to do so at counter]*
INVENTOR:	See how good my invention is?
BOSS:	I certainly do. Okay Shredder, get that Excuses Bin out of here.
UNION ORGANISER:	Quick, think of an excuse for saving yourselves.
EXCUSES BIN:	*[to Union Organiser]* That's supposed to be your job. *[to Sasha]* How about ... my sock was left behind when I was climbing in the Himalayas. And it was used as a marker during an avalanche.

The Not-So-Great Excuse Machine

ASSISTANT: That's a good excuse for losing a sock but not for keeping an Excuses Bin.

[Shredder moves Excuses Bin a little further towards exit]

EXCUSES: *[fearfully]* Quick, quick
Think of an excuse for saving ourselves.
We can't think of one.
What'll we do?

TONI: *[enters with sack labelled 'Best fruit in town.' Empties apples over the counter]* Is this the Excuse Emporium?

BOSS: Sure is. And we now have the very latest technology to help our clients. What can we do for you?

TONI: See these apples? *[holds one up]* Every apple's got a worm. Now what do I tell my customers?

LATE-HARRI: Our machine can solve that, right away

INVENTOR: *[programs machine and waits for paper to come out]* No problems. We'll have that solved for you in no time.

AEM: We suggest you tell your customers that you're offering them worms because they're high in protein and make excellent eating.

TONI: What if they don't eat meat? Lots of vegetarians around.

AEM: Tell them that the worms are provided free to be used as fishing bait.

TONI: If they don't eat meat, they probably don't eat fish either.

AEM: If that's the case, bury the worms in the garden. Worms improve the soil.

TONI: Terrific. They're such good excuses; I'll pay double your normal fee as a bonus. *[pays bill, exits carrying paper]*

UNION ORGANISER: What do you think you're doing? Negotiating a bonus is my job.

BOSS: *[pointedly ignores Union Organiser; gestures at Excuses Bin]* Right Shredder, do your job. Get those out-of-date Excuses out of here. They're past their use-by date. Make them into Ex-Excuses.

EXCUSES BIN: *[in a terrible state]*
Quick, think of an excuse for being technologically challenged.
Say we'll clog up the works.
We're the wrong kind of paper to make mulch.
Our ink will kill the flowers. And mess up the flower beds.
And then they'll only grow weeds ...
Another problem, another excuse needed.
[they wail together] Anyway, the AEM still hasn't proved itself.
And it's much too soon to send us to the Shredder.

SHREDDER: That's enough. We know what's best for you.

EXCUSES: Give us five minutes. Then we'll be Ex-Excuses.

WORRIER: *[thoughtfully]* Ex-Excuses. If X means the unknown...

LATE-HARRI: Is X the things we know we don't know?

WORRIER: Or all the things we don't know we know?

ASSISTANT:	*[knowingly]* There's a lot we don't know.
SHREDDER:	*[by now Excuses Bin is almost off stage]* That's enough. At least we know what's best for you.
QUEUE:	*[jostling to be served]* Come on, serve us now. We need excuses for chopping down a tree. Refusing to eat vegetables. Snoring at camp and keeping everyone awake. Not tidying our bedrooms. Forgetting the cat is allergic to fish. For calling my girl/boy friend by the wrong name.
	[SFX-working noise increases as Inventor tries to feed all these problems into the machine]
MILES:	*[enters with computer discs/USBs]* Is this the Excuse Emporium?
BOSS:	Sure is. We're bigger and better than ever. What's more, we have plenty of fresh stock available.
MILES:	*[holds up computer discs]* That's good, because I need an excuse for feeding my father's computer with the latest Mortal Kombat game and accidentally offloading everything on his hard disc.
INVENTOR:	Just give me a minute. *[feeds problem into AEM]*
	[SFX-machine working]
AEM:	We suggest the following excuse: Tell your father that you're an ace hacker and Bank Megalopolis needed you to fix up their system. The only way it could be done is by removing all the information on your father's hard disc.

	Unfortunately, just as you were setting up the Bank Megalopolis system, a storm passed overhead. Consequently, there was a great surge of electricity and every computer system in town broke down.
MILES:	That's wonderful. Can I use my father's bankcard to pay my bill? *[pays and leaves]*
EXCUSES:	*[by now quite frantic]* We'd never think of an excuse like that. We don't know anything about computers. We give up. *[they hide in bin]*
	[SFX-noisy weeping]
CHRIS:	*[enters carrying large heart-shaped St Valentine's Day card]* I need an excuse…
LATE-HARRI:	For St Valentine's Day?
CHRIS:	The person I like doesn't believe in romance. I bought this card and now I don't know whether to send it.
QUEUE:	Why not? That's what St Valentine's Day is all about. You don't have to sign it. There's no way he/she'll know who sent it. Keep them guessing. Some people get lots of those cards. St Valentine's Day cards cost heaps.
CHRIS:	You don't understand. She'll probably think it comes from this spunk in Year 12.
ASSISTANT:	So what if she does?
CHRIS:	But she's always giving me excuses for not wanting to be with me. What I need is an

	excuse for giving her this card so that she'll realise I'm serious about her.
INVENTOR:	*[doubtful]* Sounds romantic. I'm not sure if the AEM has been programmed for romance. We only deal in facts. Can romance fit into a binary system?
ASSISTANT:	Don't see why not. Romance is all about couples.
WORRIER:	Or not being couples. That's a worry.
BOSS:	*[worried]* Romance is important in people's lives. This machine won't be any use to us if it can't handle excuses for emotions.
EXCUSES BIN:	*[by now almost off stage]* Romantic excuses is one of our specialities. Sometimes we sell them in bulk. To people who are on their own and don't want to be. To people who want to get out of a relationship. To people who want an excuse for doing zany things.
WORRIER:	I don't understand that.
ASSISTANT:	It's really quite simple. People say they are romantics when they want an excuse for doing zany things.
BOSS:	Let's get back to business. There's a customer here who wants to buy an excuse for putting a name on a St Valentine's Day card instead of sending it anonymously.
AEM:	No file for that. It's a fact that St Valentine's Day cards are always anonymous.

CHRIS:	Being anonymous is no good to me. What I need is an excuse for love to be acknowledged.
	[SFX-of machine working hard. Paper thrown everywhere. AEM slowly and noisily falls apart.]
CHRIS:	*[watching in horror]* The machine's broken down and I still need an excuse for feeling the way I do.
EXCUSES BIN:	*[calling from the exit]* But you don't need an excuse for that. Romance can't be programmed for emotions. Many emotions such as love are irrational. Some excuses are not logical but people want to believe them. That's why we are in such demand. That's why we can't be replaced by a machine.
CHRIS:	You mean, I should just send the card and not worry about an excuse?
ASSISTANT:	Exactly. The card itself is an indication of your feelings.
BOSS:	Hey Shredder, bring that Excuse Bin right back here.
	[Shredder starts to push Bin back into centre of stage. Queue jostles around Bin]
QUEUE:	What about us? My turn to get served. I was first, I was first... We're feeling neglected. When are you going to invent some excuse cards?

INVENTOR:	*[waving arm in acknowledgment towards Excuse Bin]* Feelings are your specialty. My machine and I will stick to facts.
ASSISTANT:	Then we'll need both of you.
BOSS:	Good thinking. This way we can really handle all our business and even expand our services.
AEM:	You've heard of e-mail? Ours will be excuse-mail.
BOSS:	So instead of snail-mail, we'll have e-mail.
LATE-HARRI:	Just one more thing. We need a good ad.
QUEUE:	For the shop front window. The local paper. Radio spots. TV promos. To go on the Internet.

[everybody joins hands and sings the excuse-mail commercial, to be sung to the nursery rhyme melody of 'Who's Afraid of The Big Bad Wolf']

WHO'S IN NEED OF A GOOD EXCUSE?
A BETTER EXCUSE, THE BEST EXCUSE.
WHO'S IN NEED OF THE RIGHT EXCUSE?
TO ZAP YOUR WORRY NOW

[everyone jumps up and down]

POW!!!

Relevant issues for discussion

Some topics for discussion include:

- **Industrial relations:** Discuss how the characters get along at work when new technology arrives, and identify which workers embrace or resist the changes.
- **Negotiation skills:** Explore the different ways characters try to convince others to accept new technology, and discuss which approaches work best.
- **Small business:** Consider the tough choices the business faces when buying new technology – think about the cost, training needs, and how staff feel about it.
- **Unionisation:** Look at how workers team up to have their voices heard about the new technology, and discuss whether working together helps them.
- **The significance of new technology:** Identify the ways new technology changes how people work together, and explore both the good and bad effects on the workplace.
- **Customer service:** Compare how customers are treated with the old and new systems, and decide which method you think works better.
- **Personnel management:** Explore how the managers handle their staff during these changes, and discuss what makes a good leader when introducing new technology.

Activities

1. Dated! Initialled?

Computer discs have been replaced by USBs. And they will be replaced by something else. In some ways, asking carefully prompted questions of AI (Artificial Intelligence) has now overtaken the Automatic Excuses Machine.

If you were writing a script that you didn't want to date, what would you name the various technical/digital devices, so the script didn't sound out-dated? Would you make up a name, rather than use a real label? Q-tech? Re-Cord?

Are there any devices names known just by initials which are confusing for others? Can you think of three devices which have new names now to perform those functions like recording or photographing? (Check with older family if unsure.)

2. AI discussion starters

Here are some discussion starters. Choose the most relevant for your group.

- Can you think of an excuse why you should/should not use AI? Could AI apply to you?

- As an actor/model, your face and body image is marketable but can be cloned by CGI (Computer Generated Imagery). You are paid once and get no further work. Should you be paid for residuals each time your image is digitally used? Or is the initial fee to be your only income? Did you know this when you signed the contract for the one-off payment?

- You're part of a band. You all help create and perform the songs and music. Suddenly one of your songs becomes very popular and earns millions. The band members start to argue about who owns it. They genuinely can't remember who did what. One person negotiates a big recording contract only in their own name. Then it is copied by AI. What could happen next?

- You've created a unique recipe for a healthy, non-alcoholic drink with a distinctive taste and name. Your brand is well known. Someone does a cheaper 'knock off' recipe with a very similar name and starts to take your market. What can you do? What should you have done earlier?

- Would you buy a fake designer product which is a cheap imitation? Why? Why not?

- Many kinds of designs need protection for their originators. Maps. Plans. Prototypes. Models. Concepts. Formula. Fashions. Music. Shows. Recipes. New systems. How would you organise this if you oversaw the appropriate agency?

- Patent, watermark, copyright, trademark, licensing, royalties: what do each mean?
- How can I prevent my idea being pinched and copied by others?
- You're an engineer who has designed a new means of transport. It works brilliantly and potentially has a big market. How will you protect your idea?
- You've organised a travelling exhibition of special games, A competitor copies your concept. What can you do?
- You've developed a new biofuel from waste? Or a cancer drug? Will you offer it free? Who should pay for it and how? What if you offer it free and others sell it on at a big profit? How can you protect your gift? Or recoup the expense of your original research, which may have taken years?
- Hydroponics can be used to grow fresh vegetables on board a boat. But fresh water is needed. Some have experimented with solar panels. Find out what has worked so far? Who should get credit for these ideas?

3. The evolution of the workforce

Find out five occupations/jobs/trades which no longer exist because of innovations/new machine/tools or devices.

What replaced them?

How did those skilled in the original way cope with the new ways of working?

Any strikes? Protests? Re-training?

Historically, who were the Luddites?

Old or 'sunset' jobs: How many have you heard before?

Here are some to discuss:

- SANDWICHMAN: A bloke who wears a sandwich billboard for advertising

- APOTHECARY: Someone who prepared and sold medicines or drugs; now chemist
- HABERDASHER: Dealer in small wares; tapes, pins needles, thread, linen. (Formerly also hats)
- NIGHT MAN/HONEY DIPPER: Collected dunny waste from outside dunnies; a bloke who empties the dunny can from outhouses
- INTERPRETER: A person who translates between languages on the spot (being replaced by AI translation tech)
- SHORTHAND TYPIST: A person who takes dictation in shorthand and types it up
- VIDEO SHOP WORKER: A person who ran the local video hire shop and looked after the tapes and discs
- ANIMATOR: Artist who drew animation cells by hand (mostly replaced by computer animation)
- PUSH MOWER OPERATOR: Bloke who mowed lawns with a manual mower
- BOOKKEEPER: Professional who did the books and recorded money matters by hand
- ARMOURER: Made suits of armour or plates of armour for buildings or ships etc.
- AWL BLADE MAKER: Craftsman who made metal tools for leather work, mainly used by saddlers and cobblers
- BALER: A person who bales hay. In the mills one who baled wool or cotton goods
- BARBER SURGEON: A barber who also acted as a surgeon (an Act was passed that limited Barbers to hair-cutting, shaving, dentistry and blood letting in the 18th century)
- BULLOCKY: A term for the driver of a bullock team (Australian)
- CLOGGER: Maker of wooden shoes – clogs

Everyperson

A classroom play for secondary students

A playscript of approximately 40 minutes performance time

Rationale

A parody is a work that mimics the style of another work, artist, or genre in an exaggerated way, usually for comic effect.

The casino parody is based on the updated concept of the medieval morality play Everyman, where the protagonist is faced with crucial life choices. Instead of virtues and vices, Everyperson must make choices among symbolic cards in this Casino of Life where the currency is time, not money. The script demands from players and audience an original ending which requires rational choices. The skills of logic as well as dramatic construction are required to finish the play in an appropriate way. The play poses fundamental questions such as: Which cards should Everyperson play? What does each represent in terms of 'life values'? The ethics of gambling is an issue which will need to be discussed.

Outline

Everyperson is gambling on a generic card game at the Casino of Life, because nothing is going right. The Croupier deals Everyperson a 'living' card hand. Dialogue occurs between Everyperson and the cards. Each card, which represents a concept, tries to persuade Everyperson to spend time in its province.

- Queen of Hearts attempts to appeal to Everyperson's desire to live beyond the mundane
- King of Diamonds insists that money be first priority
- Nine of Hearts cautions that without a visit to the game of health, nothing will be enjoyed
- Eight of Clubs insists that the fame game requires total commitment to work
- Jack of Spades claims death solves everything
- The Joker speaks in apparent riddles, but with wise comments

Each character introduces itself and connection to the Casino of Life. A fire alarm causes an emergency evacuation and enables Everyperson to rescue the pack. The Narrator then offers the audience the opportunity to decide the future of Everyperson. Indirectly, the audience is choosing its own fate.

Cast

Severals parts can be played by any gender.

The Card Chorus can be expanded or contracted to allow for more or fewer parts.

- NARRATOR
- CROUPIER
- EVERYPERSON
- QUEEN OF HEARTS: ROMANCE
- KING OF DIAMONDS: WEALTH
- NINE OF HEARTS: HEALTH
- EIGHT OF CLUBS: FAME

- JACK OF SPADES: DEATH
- JOKER: THE WISE FOOL
- CARD CHORUS
- DICE

Props and costumes

- Each character wears sandwich board or T-shirt with appropriate symbol
- Tables
- Chairs
- Mock-up poker machines
- Empty wallet

Sound effects (SFX)

- Tinny sound of coins falling to indicate wins
- Flashing lights
- Background songs such as 'Luck, be a lady tonight' etc.
- Drum roll
- Fire siren

Setting

- The interior of a casino
- Table and chairs set into the centre of the stage
- Row of Poker Machines at back of stage

Script

NARRATOR: *[steps out in front of stage]* Welcome to the Casino of Life. Here we play the Decision Game.
Everyone welcome. Free parking. Complimentary drinks. Open 24 hours a day.

EVERYPERSON: *[enters from stage left]* Am I in the right place?

CROUPIER: Depends on what you want to risk. Time or money? In most casinos you play with money. Here, you play with time, your own. Minutes, hours, days, and even years. You can risk your whole life. What are you prepared to risk?

EVERYPERSON: Risk? Everything. Nothing in my life's going right. My lover's just left and I've lost my job. I owe heaps on my bankcard...

NARRATOR: *[carelessly]* That kind of stuff can happen to anyone...

EVERYPERSON: Hang on, I haven't finished yet. My team's just dropped me and I can't get rid of this hay fever. *[sneezes loudly]*

CROUPIER: *[turning away]* No point you coming in here. The aim is to leave here with a balanced hand. You haven't got anything to gamble with.

EVERYPERSON: What's wrong with me? I'll gamble on myself. I'm sure I've got something to offer.

NARRATOR: The Casino of Life offers choices. A whole pack of choices. You spend time here and work out how you want to spend it elsewhere. Let me introduce you to my pack.

CARD CHORUS: *[march on in suites]*

	We're the hearts.
	We're the spades.
	We're the diamonds.
	We're the clubs.
EVERYPERSON:	Apart from being cards, what are you? *[each card steps forward in turn]*
QUEEN OF HEARTS:	I'm the Queen of Hearts. I am Romance with a capital R.
EVERYPERSON:	You mean, like love and stuff?
QUEEN OF HEARTS:	Yes, but lots more. I am Adventure, Fantasy and Imagination. Without me, there would be no dreaming in your life.
EVERYPERSON:	Daydreams or nightmares?
KING OF DIAMONDS:	*[swaggers to front of stage]* I'm the King of Diamonds. Though I don't need to introduce myself. I put the sparkle in life. My wealth enables you to buy time.
DICE:	*[rolling and shaking, picking up on each other's sentences]* Time payment? Watch out for players like him. Spend too much now, long term you don't win. *[they roll off stage]*
EVERYPERSON:	*[pulls out empty wallet and shakes it]* I'm almost broke.
NINE OF HEARTS:	*[acts like a fitness trainer, runs on the spot, etc]* You don't need wealth to be fit. I'm the Nine of Hearts. I am Health. Rich or poor, you'll need me. I always fit in.

EVERYPERSON:	*[sneezes loudly]* You reckon? I've still got the flu.
NINE OF HEARTS:	See? Proves how much you need me.
CROUPIER:	This is like an introduction agency. I match up needs. Next …
EIGHT OF CLUBS:	I'm Fame. No need to be introduced. I'm so well known.
EVERYPERSON:	So who are you?
DICE:	Give Everyperson five minutes of fame. That's enough.
EVERYPERSON:	Why introduce them to me?
CARD CHORUS:	Because you need most of us for more than five minutes.
EVERYPERSON:	Do I get to choose who or when? How many am I allowed in a hand?
NARRATOR:	As many as you need. You've already made some of those choices. That's why you're here.
JOKER:	*[acts like a clown]* I'm the joker in the pack. I confuse and bemuse. Sometimes I refuse.
EVERYPERSON:	What does that mean?
JOKER:	Wise or foolish, Joker or seer. I make both clear.
	[All cards strike poses. Some do handstands.]
JOKER:	Turn it up or turn it down. Throw it out, or send it round.
CROUPIER:	*[aside to audience]* They're a hard lot to control.

	[to Everyperson] Okay, okay. Time to deal your hand. Cards, do your shuffle.
	[cards do a shuffling interweaving dance and freeze!]
DICE:	*[tumbling back on stage]* What about us?
NARRATOR:	Wrong time, wrong place. This is a card game. Come back for two-up or Snakes and Ladders.
DICE:	*[leave in a huff]* Not in a casino. We get thrown around everywhere.
EVERYPERSON:	Do I pick the cards to go in my hand?
CROUPIER:	Of course. If you gamble in an ordinary casino, you have no control. Most people lose. Here, you must show skill in choosing which cards will determine your life. Your chances are better. You may even win.
EVERYPERSON:	Win against whom? Who is my opponent?
NARRATOR:	Boredom. Dullness. A wasted life. Didn't you realise? Once you stepped in that door, you'd made the decision to play in the Game of Life. And here, the odds aren't stacked against you. Choose well and live well. Choose badly and suffer.
EVERYMAN:	*[cards step out as selected]* I choose Fame, Health, Wealth and Romance. How many more am I allowed?
JOKER:	Whichever you choose won't be enough; you'll forget the other important stuff.
	[SFX-roll of drums, stage darkens]
ACE OF SPADES:	I never get chosen, but I'm always in the pack.

CARD CHORUS:	*[shrink away from Ace, Joker's teeth chatter]* The Ace of Spades! Death! Keep him away from us.
JOKER:	Hey, it's not the end of the game…
ACE OF SPADES:	… you'll come to me, just the same.
CROUPIER:	The game begins. The rules are as follows; the House plays the first card. Everyperson must choose a card to match the House. Some cards are worth more than others.
EVERYPERSON:	How do I know which are the best cards?
DICE:	You'll only know by playing.
CROUPIER:	The House plays card 1. *[a card steps out from the crowd]*
EVERYPERSON:	Okay, okay. I choose Diamonds to throw first.
CROUPIER:	Bad choice. This round goes to the House. *[they play a few rounds]*
EVERYPERSON:	*[excitedly]* I'm winning. Again! *[cards jump up and down, cast dances around stage]*
JOKER:	*[warningly]* Just luck. You believe, it's luck when you're winning And fate when you're not.
CARDS:	Be quiet, you fool!
JOKER:	I'm entitled to my point of view. Don't think I'm just a fool. I'm the chorus that speaks in rhyme. Comments on action, and warns you in time. But I'm the wise one playing the fool. What I show you is really cool.

NARRATOR:	*[claps hands, steps out in front of stage]* Now it's time to create your own ending to this script. There are several ways of doing this. Perhaps each of the cast wants it to end differently. They've always had minds of their own.
	[SFX-loud fire siren]
CROUPIER:	Fire! Everybody out of the building. Don't use the lifts. Down the fire-escape.
CARD CHORUS:	*[mill around frantically]* Protect us. We're cardboard. If the flames get to us, we'll go up in smoke.
	[Everyperson scoops up pack and pushes them off stage]
NARRATOR:	This is a dramatic moment. What happens next? Let the play finish the way the players wish. Comedy or tragedy? It's up to you. *[gestures to cast and audience]* Should the ending be happy or sad?
	[cards step forward in turn]
KING OF DIAMONDS:	Choose me and my way of thinking. Casinos are to do with people's dreams of money. If you see life my way, owning things is the only thing that matters. If the play ends the way I think it should, then Everyperson should hold me in the final hand.
EVERYPERSON:	Maybe. But if I hadn't helped you down the stairs, you would have gone up in smoke.
QUEEN OF HEARTS:	*[pushes King of Diamonds aside]* What's the point of owning things if you've no one to share it with? Family, friends and lovers; that's what makes life complete. Anyway, if you don't

	use me, your life will be totally boring. Make the ending fit my way of thinking.
EVERYPERSON:	Ho hum. Takes a fire to find out who your real friends are.
NINE OF HEARTS:	No point having friends if you don't work out. You'll never have enough energy to play with them. My way of thinking is a fitting way to end any play.
EVERYPERSON:	*[clasps hands with Nine of Hearts]* Right you are. I'll have to hand it to you.
EIGHT OF CLUBS:	While you're working out, you won't have time to join the fame game. Total commitment, that's what I demand. Count me in.
JACK OF SPADES:	*[butts in]* Good. You'll get all exhausted and come to me even faster. Death solves everything. Can be timely, untimely, accidental, preventable, or an appropriate end to a fully lived life.
NARRATOR:	Stop interrupting. This audience has heard enough from you to make up their own minds. Let them decide how to play the last act.
DICE:	You mean, the last hand.
CARD CHORUS excluding JOKER:	That's us. We're fifty-two cards in search of a life.
JOKER:	Hey, how about me? Don't be a fool. Count me in, too.
EVERYPERSON:	Perhaps the audience will suggest a solution. *[turns to audience]* What would you do?

Ending

1. Members of the audience to pick the cards (maximum five) they decide to keep.
2. Give reasons for each choice.
3. Decide the fate of Everyperson at the end of the game. Will Everyperson leave the Casino of Life with a balanced hand or empty handed? Will anyone accompany Everyperson?
4. Will the Joker have the last word (in rhyme)? Or will the Narrator close the scene?
5. What is the final role of the Ace of Spades in the Casino of Life?
6. A possible solution might be a balance of the four suites and the Joker.

Relevant issues for discussion

Some relevant topics for discussion include:

- **Making significant choices and discussion guidelines:**
  - What is my problem?
  - What are my options?
  - What are the likely outcomes?
  - What is the best that can happen?
  - What is the worst that can happen? How can I handle this?
  - How might my actions affect others?
  - How much should I take others' circumstances into consideration?
- **Probability theory:** Is there such a thing as luck? Or is it possible to influence your own future by the decisions and actions you take? Is your future predetermined?
  - What are the odds on winning?
  - How many people lose far too much?
  - Why do people rationalise their losses and say, 'Next time'?
- **Risk:** Why do people use terms like 'investing' instead of 'risking'? What's the difference between a calculated risk and gambling? Why is 'risk-taker' a complimentary label, and 'gambler' derogatory?

- **Gamling:** What's the difference between an entrepreneur and a gambler? (An entrepreneur is attempting to build a business, and to produce tangible products that people can use. A gambler is merely trying to make money.) Are there different types of gambling? Where skill is involved? Some where it's just luck? For example, checking a racing form guide, versus relying on the one-armed bandits (poker machines)?

Activities

1. Parodies

A parody is a work that mimics the style of another work, artist, or genre in an exaggerated way, usually for comic effect.

Choose a well-known song or poem and make up a parody, using a different subject which is relevant to your audience.

Some ideas include:

- A TV commercial
- A song for your sports team.

2. Entitled

This script is called 'Everyperson'. The morality play which inspired it was called 'Everyman'. A title should point out the main ideas, threads or themes in the script.

Making choices in how you spend your time, instead of your money. This is one idea-thread.

Rename the script.

The Fairly Fake TV Show

A satirical 'Whodunnit' for the classroom

A playscript of approximately 40 minutes performance time

Rationale

The conventions of a 'whodunnit' are familiar to most audiences. Whereas, in a satire, a serious subject may be trivialised or inverted, or a trivial subject ridiculed through exaggeration. The aim is to make the audience think differently about a familiar or everyday experience. And maybe suggest a solution. Some TV chat shows give intimate topics the status of an international issue. Thus they lend themselves to being satirised.

Outline

The top-ranking 'Fairley Fake' TV show allows selected guests to chat about issues and people in their lives. The program thrives on controversy. Previous topics have caused many letters and phone calls of response, both in favour and against the program.

Today's audience of animals is eager to comment on Anima-Therapy: The Relationship of Animals and Their Pet-Persons. The program is live-to-air.

Fairley's make-up is finished, the audience is warmed up and the show begins. Halfway through the show, Fairley dies after sipping coffee. It's not a heart attack. Fairley doesn't have one.

Was she poisoned? Intentionally? Or by accident? And if so, what was the motive? Who did it? Was it a disgruntled fan? Was it a colleague or a crew member? Or was it the spouse, friend or relative of a tell-all contestant?

A bloodhound begins to investigate.

Cast

Several parts can be played by any gender. Several parts can be spoken by one person; for example audience and ad person, Fairley Fake and Bloodhound.

Minimum cast: 10

Maximum cast: 25 plus

- FAIRLEY FAKE (FF): Off camera, FF is bad-tempered, jealous and vindictive.
- ASSISTANT: Clever, but frustrated in ambition to have own show.
- MAKE-UP ARTIST: Wears outrageous outfit.
- ROVER: Dog-guest with job as security guard.
- TOM: A 15-year-old pet-person.
- SILVA: Siamese cat.
- BAMBI: A 15-year-old pet-person.
- ASTRA: Astrologer/weatherperson.
- AD PERSON: Wears a business suit has longer speeches than other characters.
- SHOW'S DIRECTOR: Worldly wise but weary.

- BLOODHOUND: Clever investigator, wears Sherlock Holmes hat, carries magnifying glass and notebook.
- AUDIENCE: Fans, animals wearing FF Fan T-shirts.
- OPTIONAL NON-SPEAKING PARTS: technicians, camera operators, security guard.

Props

- 2 coffee mugs, one labelled FF
- Small and giant cue cards with FF written on the back
- Microphone
- TV cameras
- TV monitor
- TV lights
- Make-up
- Make-up mirror
- Isolation booth
- Magnifying glass
- Notebook
- Cap for astrologer/weatherperson
- Ratings sheet
- Fan letters
- Sherlock Holmes hat for FF

Sound effects (SFX)

One person is responsible for sound effects:

- ad music
- sounds of drinking, rattling cups etc.

Setting

- TV studio with an isolation booth to one side

Script

[Assistant and Director are centre stage]

ASSISTANT: *[holding mobile microphone]* Welcome to the Fairley Fake Show. The chat show where we solve a million relationship problems.

[Audience, depending on numbers, are seated on one side or to the front. They cheer, clap, make various animal noises, e.g. barks, whistles, quacks, miaows, growls, etc.]

ASSISTANT: We deal in passion here. Does Fate determine love, hate, even despair for you ... and your pet person?

[louder cheers, noises and claps from the Audience]

ASSISTANT: Your pet-person's lifestyle, his or her astrological chart, and even the spiritual path to Nirvana are the subject of today's program. *[more Audience response]* And here's the host of today's show ... welcome to our one and only, the first and final Fairley Fake.

[enter FF carrying coffee mug]
[Audience goes wild]
[Make-Up Artist rushes in with giant powder puff and dusts everyone]

DIRECTOR: *[complaining]* Hey, I'm not even on camera!

MAKE-UP ARTIST: *[dusting self]* Don't panic. It's not flea powder.

FF: *[snarls at Make-Up Artist in undertone]* Don't worry about them, do me.
[beams at camera, drops mug which breaks]
Quick, where's my signature mug?

	[Assistant searches for another, hands it to her]
FF:	*[to Audience]* Welcome, welcome. And how is everyone today?
DIRECTOR:	*[scratching]* Itching to go.
FF:	How can you be more spiritually in tune with your pet-person? Is the time you spend together quality time? Do you and your pet-person ever meditate together? Have you ever spent a day in their shoes? Does your pet-person lead a dog's life?
AUDIENCE:	*[intermixed with animal noises]* What about my DJ? My electrician's all wired up. My plumber just hangs around. Our house hasn't even got a kennel. They don't meditate at our place, they just sleep.
FF:	*[shushes Audience, reads off small cue card]* The focus of today's program is Anima-Therapy: The Relationship of Animals and Their Pet-Persons. Some might call it pet-tales. Our studio guests include pets and their troubled pet-persons.
ASSISTANT:	*[gesturing towards booth]* Pet-persons are invited to wait in our isolation booth. Our pets are joining us now. *[Rover and Silva walk on stage]*
FF:	But just before we begin, let's hear it from our sponsors. *[SFX-upbeat marching music]*

AD PERSON:	Does your person need regular exercising? Are they too stressed to play? Tap our double 8 number and order the PET-CISE machine to improve your owner's heartbeat. We take 'petexpress' cards. Use PET-CISE, guaranteed by our rich and famous pets. Last offer this month.
FF:	And thank you PET-CISE. The exercise machine used by the rich and famous. Now let's welcome our first guest ... give Rover a big hand er ... paw.
	[Rover comes forward. Meanwhile Silva slides in between Audience. Audience responds.]
AUDIENCE:	What do you think you're doing? Get lost! Lay off, will you? Grrrr!!! Growl!!!!
FF:	Sit, Rover. *[Rover sits]* Rover works as a security guard at 30 Station Street. Rover owns a 15-year old red-haired male called Tom. Rover's problem is that Tom spends all his time playing computer games or going out with his girlfriend. He always uses wheels, never walks. So poor Rover is ... walk-needy.
ASSISTANT:	*[aside]* We're going to have a slight communication problem here.
FF:	Huh!!! What do you mean?
ROVER:	Bark, bark
ASSISTANT:	*[to FF]* See what I mean? *[to Rover]* Was that a yes?
ROVER:	Bark, bark

ASSISTANT:	So that means two barks for yes, and one for no. Do you need a microphone, Rover?
ROVER:	Bark, bark
ASSISTANT:	That's settled then. *[holds microphone near dog]*
FF:	*[to assistant]* If I can only ask questions which have a yes or no answer, I'll need bigger cue cards.
ASSISTANT:	*[hands FF giant cue cards]* Here they are. I did all my preparations last night for today's special program.
FF:	*[nastily]* Got your eye on my job again, have you? *[remembers Audience]* Now Rover, can you count? If I ask you how many walks you get each week, can you bark the number?
ROVER:	Bark, bark
FF:	Is that two walks or is it a yes?
ROVER:	Bark, bark.
ASSISTANT:	I think we still have a communication problem here.
FF:	*[turns on Director]* It's your fault. You chose the topic. Remember the time you tried to interview that guru who only spoke in nursery rhymes?
ASSISTANT:	Do I ever. All he did was sing 'Baa, baa black sheep' and 'Three blind mice, three blind mice,' to any question asked.
DIRECTOR:	I never did work out what he was on about. But it made great publicity. He was reported

on every other channel as being racist and insulting the visually impaired.

[Rover joins Silva, both sniff around Audience]

DIRECTOR: *[sulkily from off centre]* It seemed like a good idea ... at the time.

FF: All the good ideas are mine.

ASSISTANT: Because you always blame everyone else when things go wrong.

MAKE-UP ARTIST: Or me when you look ugly. *[disapprovingly]* Expects miracles, she does.

[Rover wanders over to FF, begins to lift hind leg. Just in time Assistant yanks dog out of range.]

ASSISTANT: You never thank me for the times I save you from disaster.

MAKE-UP ARTIST: Or the times I make you look glamorous!

DIRECTOR: Or when I give you a salary raise.

FF: Of course not. That's your responsibility. *[Audience becoming restless]* Is that dog in position?

ROVER: *[wags tail]* Bark, bark.

FF: We have a surprise for Rover. Tom, Rover's pet person, is in our isolation booth. He cannot hear the questions we ask Rover. And he will not hear Rover's replies. *[to Assistant]* So what's the first question?

ASSISTANT: *[reads]* Rover is a walk-needy dog. Rover, how many times has your pet-person Tom taken you for a walk this week?

[Rover sits wagging his tail]

FF: How many times is that? Rover, did you understand the question?

ROVER: Bark, bark.

ASSISTANT: I think he's saying he didn't have any walks.

FF: But he barked twice. Doesn't that mean two walks? Luckily here's our astrologer/weather-person to help us understand. Let's welcome Astra to give us the latest weather report and read the future for the pet-person relationship between Rover and Tom.

ASTRA: *[blesses the audience]* May the fur, feather and fins be with you. A cold front approaching early in the day with a few thundery showers.

FF: Yes, Astra, thank you for that. Now I'd like to ask Tom to join us. *[Audience boos, hisses, FF holds up warning hand]* Let's not blame Tom for the lack of walks ... yet.

[Tom comes out; more boos, hisses]

TOM: *[looks sheepish]* I thought Rover and I had a good relationship. I mean ... I always feed him on time.

ROVER: Bark.

TOM: er ... I was a bit late once.

ROVER: Bark, bark.

TOM: And during last week's storm, I didn't let him come inside; even though I knew he was scared of lightning.

FF: Why wouldn't you let him in?

TOM: I couldn't. Mum would've killed me. The carpets had just been shampooed.

FF: What about walks? Rover claims you don't take him on walks. That's a serious fault in a relationship such as yours. You need quality time together.

TOM: Well, I've been studying. And there's my girlfriend, and …

FF: *[sternly]* Do you ever meditate together?

TOM: With Rover? We don't even speak the same language. He's only interested in walks, bones, digging holes in Mum's garden and chasing cats.

FF: Let's see what Astra suggests.

ASTRA: *[very seriously]* A pet-person relationship is a very special one. Understanding is needed on both sides. Perhaps there could be short walks with varied smells near bigger trees. Try one tomorrow. By then, this low should have passed over. Fine weather is expected.

TOM: *[rather doubtfully]* You think?

ASTRA: I'm hardly ever wrong with the weather. And as for dogs, Rover is very faithful, and would not consider another pet-person. Do you feel the same way about him?

TOM: I suppose so. He chose me from the Lost People's Home.

ASTRA: Now I'll put on my astrologer's cap *[does this]* and consider your star signs. Of course, Rover is Sirius, the dog star. And that's not the best

	sign to be matched with Aquarius, a water sign. Aquarians are free spirits. They don't like being attached to anybody.
FF:	A watery sign. How interesting. Can you swim, Tom?
TOM:	Of course. In summer I'm a lifesaver.
FF:	Can you swim, Rover?
ROVER:	Bark, bark.
AUDIENCE:	*[joins in with various animal noises]* Hate getting my fur wet I'm all for more bird baths Frogs need bigger ponds Mud, mud glorious mud ...
FF:	*[silences audience with a stern look]* So where do you see this relationship going? Straight back to the kennel? Is Rover just to be tossed a bone? Or is the relationship going forward swimmingly? *[loud groan from Audience]* After this message from our sponsors, the audience will offer its advice to Rover and Tom. *[SFX-fast-paced computer-style music]*
AD PERSON:	Try the Pet-Equette Hot-Line, the latest computer matching service for pets. Key in your tastes in food, exercise, games, kennels, cages and fish bowls for a perfect match. Do you want a pet-person who is short or tall, light or heavy build with a flea-safe medical certificate? For a deep and meaningful relationship, paw print your international Pet-Express and join Pet-Equette NOW!

[SFX-more fast-paced computer-style music]

FF: Welcome back to the subject of today's program: Anima-Therapy: The Relationship of Animals and Their Pet-Persons. And now it's time for the audience to advise Rover and Tom on their relationship.

[Assistant walks into audience holding microphone while FF sips from coffee mug. Tom stands there, looking stupid.]

AUDIENCE: *[animal noises interspersed]*
Rover, why not nip his heels? Yes, get Torm moving.
You're not pulling on the leash hard enough.
Try whining. Tom's folks will force him to take you out of earshot, then.
If he does take you on a walk, don't stop at every tree.
Above all Rover, don't chase cats.

FF: That's excellent advice. Did you hear that, Rover?

ROVER: Bark, bark.

FF: Does that mean, yes yes? *[hurriedly, before Rover can bark again]* What advice does the audience have for his pet-person?

AUDIENCE: Get off your bike, Tom!
Walk the dog, man.
Get the girlfriend to walk with you. Take Rover to the beach.
Try surfing.

ROVER: Bark, bark.

FF: Did everybody hear that? Rover and Tom, you are in danger of ruining a close relationship. Rover, when you next take Tom for a walk, make sure Tom's leash isn't left too tight. Leave room for some individuality.

ASTRA: Can I also suggest a counselling session, cut rates of course for all Fairley Fake Fans, tomorrow morning, in my offices? Tomorrow, of course, will be warm and sunny.

ROVER: Bark, bark.

FF: Thank you, Astra. Have you ever been wrong?

ASTRA: Never for the weather. Nor for anything else. At least, not in public.

FF: Let's hear it for Tom and Rover.

[Audience claps, makes animal noises. Tom and Rover walk off centre just as Make-Up Artist returns to powder everybody on stage.]

FF: Our next guest has an intimate relationship problem. To do with smells. *[checks cue card]* Our pet claims that her pet-person wears too much perfume. Let's hear a welcome for Silva ... the Siamese cat ... a part-time catwalk model.

[Audience claps and cheers as Silva slinks on]

SILVA: Miaow.

FF: *[reading from cue card]* Silva communicates only by thoughts. However, highly intelligent brains can pick up those waves. *[hisses to Director]* I can't understand what this cat is on about.

SILVA:	Miaow, miaow. *[smiles serenely at Audience]*
DIRECTOR:	*[brushing all this aside]* Silva thinks that her pet person, Bambi, spends too much on perfume, deodorant and make-up. She should just wash herself like all cats do. Grooming should be a personal habit. Not a multi-national marketing exercise.
FF:	She thinks all that?
ASSISTANT:	Those are just some of her thoughts. She's on fast forward today.
FF:	Tell her to think in slow motion.
ASSISTANT:	That might be too fast for this program.
FF:	*[to Assistant]* Obviously a catty remark. *[to Audience]* Let's have an ad from our sponsors.
	[SFX-uplifting music]
AD PERSON:	For a small monthly outlay, you can be the proud owner of a new face. Try the Full Catastrophe Whisker Lift. No drooping tail, no dull fur. Add more pep to your nine lives. Try the new look the Whole Catastrophe.
	[SFX-more uplifting music]
FF:	And back to our program on Anima-Therapy: The Relationship of ... Ohhhh. *[FF suddenly drops to the floor. Director, Assistant, Tom and Bambi rush to her. Director tries to give her the 'kiss of life.']*
TOM:	Has she fainted?
ASTRA:	Is she having a heart attack?

ASSISTANT: Can't be. She doesn't have one.

BAMBI: Is she dead?

[Make-Up Artist checks pulse, holds mirror to lips, shakes head]

DIRECTOR: Is that a yes or a no?

ROVER: Bark, bark.

ASSISTANT: Yes?

AUDIENCE: *[terribly upset]*
What happened?
Did she have a stroke?
It must've been a heart attack.
Maybe she was murdered?
Is the program axed? Now I'll never get on.
But we'll be on the 6 o'clock news.

ASSISTANT: We're still on air. Quick, cross to our sponsors.

[SFX-funereal march]

AD PERSON: Pets, have you prepaid your funeral? Don't leave your grieving pet-person with a financial problem. Deposit funds in our grief bank. You can trust our counsellors to handle all your requirements with discretion. Pay now and die later.

AUDIENCE: *[Indignant]*
What bad taste! What bad timing!
Will Fairley get a discount? Someone call an ambulance. Someone call the police.

[Bloodhound walks on stage from audience]

BLOODHOUND: This is serious. It isn't a media mock-up. Fairley is dead. This is real life. This isn't a fake.

	No one is to leave this stage. Audience, stay in your seats.
	[shocked Audience and crew do as told]
ASSISTANT:	*[to Bloodhound]* Who do you think you are?
	[Bloodhound hands Director his card]
ASSISTANT:	*[reads over Director's shoulder]* A. Blood. PhD of SCD.
DIRECTOR:	What do those letters mean?
BLOODHOUND:	They're my qualifications. That's a Doctorate in Sniffing and Clue Detecting.
BAMBI:	Who do you work for?
BLOODHOUND:	This channel. Ms Fake had been receiving ... certain letters.
ASSISTANT:	She got sacks of letters. And e-mails.
BLOODHOUND:	But these letters were anonymous. And threats were made.
ASTRA:	My stars tell me those letters were death threats.
BLOODHOUND:	Obviously. Why else would I be here? There's always a motive for murder.
SILVA:	Miaow, miaow. Absolutely.
BAMBI:	*[astonished]* Silva? I didn't know you could talk.
SILVA:	Miaow, miaow. There's a lot you don't know about me.
BLOODHOUND:	*[pulls out notepad]* Naturally, I've been snooping around. 'How', 'why' and 'who' are

	the important questions. In cluey terms, we're talking of motive, means and opportunity. I need to talk to each of you in turn. Who's first. Any volunteers?
	[everybody on stage pushes others forward] *[Audience in uproar]*
AUDIENCE:	You go first. No way. It was your idea to come here. I suspect I'm a suspect. That means I am too.
BLOODHOUND:	*[shouts]* Quiet. *[everybody falls silent]* Director, do you have a list of everyone on this set?
DIRECTOR:	Yes. I've got the crew listed, and today's guests ...
MAKE-UP ARTIST:	Are on my list.
BLOODHOUND:	Do you want to be first?
MAKE-UP ARTIST:	Why not? I didn't do it.
BLOODHOUND:	You said 'it'. What did you mean by it?
MAKE-UP ARTIST:	Getting rid of Fairley.
ASSISTANT:	But Fairley hated you. She was trying to put you off the show. You should never have told her to have a face-lift.
MAKE-UP ARTIST:	*[sulkily]* I was only trying to help. I didn't know she was trying to get me sacked until later.
BLOODHOUND:	Where were you when Fairley collapsed?
MAKE-UP ARTIST:	In the make-up room. I went back for more powder. Fairley liked her make-up retouched each ad break.

BLOODHOUND: Right. Now who's next?

ASSISTANT: Me. I was expected to have everything ready for Fairley, even before she needed it. Cue cards. Coffee.

BLOODHOUND: Coffee? Look. *[holds magnifying glass next to fallen mug]* There's a coffee mug near the body.

DIRECTOR: Fairley's signature mug. But it couldn't have been the coffee. That's too much like an Agatha Christie murder mystery.

BLOODHOUND: You're right. Fairley was your star. How did you get on with her?

DIRECTOR: All right, I suppose.

ASSISTANT: But wasn't Fairley your ex?

TOM: Ex what?

BAMBI: Ex-girlfriend. I read about it in 'TV Star' at the dentist.

DIRECTOR: Those magazines are just about prehistoric.

MAKE-UP ARTIST: Her story. Or his story?

BLOODHOUND: *[to Director]* I don't think you're telling me everything. According to my notes, Fairley had upset the sponsors, gone over budget, insulted everybody on the set and antagonised Mrs Massively Rich, the producer of this show.

BAMBI: *[looks at Silva and gets a thought]* Why does it have to be one of us. What about the audience?

AUDIENCE: *[in uproar]* But we loved Fairley.

ASSISTANT: Which Fairley did you love? The TV star? The person you read about in the 'TV Star' …

DIRECTOR:	Or the real person?
AUDIENCE:	*[confused and all talking at once]* What's the difference?
BAMBI:	The real Fairley's dead. But tomorrow, someone else will fill her role.
MAKE-UP ARTIST:	Right. I can make anyone look like a star for this program.
ASSISTANT:	But you need to have star quality. Fairley might have been difficult to work with, but she was a star act. At least, her fans thought so. *[holds up letters]* Look at all these. And they only came in yesterday. Plus emails.
AUDIENCE:	Bet my letter is in there. I sent her a rose. I sent her a herbal love potion. I recorded her a song. I e-mailed her a poem.
BLOODHOUND:	And someone sent her a death threat. All of you here had an opportunity. Most of you seem to have motives. It's the means that's the problem. How was she killed? *[checks body without touching]*
ASSISTANT:	Might it have been an accident? Remember when Fairley sliced herself on that star-shaped letter opener which was a gift from a fan?
MAKE-UP ARTIST:	Do I ever. Took me ages to clean up the blood.
TOM:	What are you going to do without her?
DIRECTOR:	*[unhappily]* Nothing much. The ratings came out this morning. We're so low, we're off the bottom of the chart. You can't even see us. The

AUDIENCE:	sponsors have pulled out, the producer is fed up, and everybody is out of a job.
	Oh, no. What will we watch? How will we fill our lunchtimes? Who will tell us what to think? Without Fairley, our relationships will collapse. Without Fairley, we'll never manage.
BLOODHOUND:	*[to Director]* Did Fairley know the show was closing down?
DIRECTOR:	Does it matter, now?
BLOODHOUND:	The police will soon be here. Until then, I'd like to check out the studio audience. *[produces a magnifying glass and proceeds to use it on the Audience]*
	[Audience responds with snarls and growls]
SILVA:	Calls himself a Bloodhound. A bit out of date. He shouldn't be touching anything until the crime scene police have finished. Hasn't he heard of forensic science and DNA matching?
ASSISTANT:	Sometimes I watch forensic science on the Open University channel.
SILVA:	Miaow. Exactly my kind of channel.
BLOODHOUND:	Now who haven't I interviewed yet? *[consults his notebook]* Tom and Rover, where were you when Fairley collapsed?
ROVER:	Bark, bark, bark.
ASSISTANT:	Three barks. Must be a warning.
BAMBI:	Or a confession.

SILVA:	That doesn't mean anything. Doesn't matter where they were then. Some poisons take a very long time to work. And they stay in the body.
TOM:	*[steps forward]* I've an admission to make. Rover and me, we were paid ...
AUDIENCE:	To commit murder?
ROVER:	Bark.
TOM:	*[indignantly]* Of course not. We were paid to say outrageous things. Whichever guest got the most boos and claps from the audience was promised a bonus.
BAMBI:	You too? That's not fair. *[walks away in a huff]*
BLOODHOUND:	How were you to be paid?
AUDIENCE:	In biscuits? Bones? Seed? Fish?
TOM:	Money. Or a year's supply of pet food.
BLOODHOUND:	That's bribery. That's a different crime from murder or manslaughter.
ROVER:	Bark, bark.
ASSISTANT:	That means yes.
BLOODHOUND:	Bribery is an unlikely motive for murder. It's time we checked on Fairley's movements from when she stepped onto this stage until she died.
DIRECTOR:	They're all on camera. Just run the monitor.

[everyone gathers around TV screen]

ASTRA: No one's doing anything out of the ordinary.

BLOODHOUND: Did Fairley touch or taste anything different?

ASSISTANT: No, just her usual non-stop coffee.

[SFX-loud sounds of people slurping coffee, teaspoons knocking against cups, etc]

AD PERSON: *[steps forward]* Are you bored by your breakfast cup? Does your life need a lift? Drink Cappuccino Tropicana. Try the new Coffee with just a taste of tropical fruit and nuts.

[SFX-more sounds of spoons, cups rattling]

MAKE-UP ARTIST: Didn't you realise that was fake too? Fairley's coffee was just coloured water with froth on top. Real cappuccino made her throw up.

DIRECTOR: Don't say that. Coffee Galore is our biggest sponsor. Ah, our ex-sponsor now …

ASSISTANT: *[holds up FF's mug]* Anyway, isn't this my mug?

BLOODHOUND: *[takes coffee mug from Assistant, sniffs it]* Smells like real coffee to me. And I can smell almonds.

BAMBI: That's the smell of Cappuccino Tropicana.

BLOODHOUND: It also could be cyanide.

AUDIENCE: *[talk among themselves]*
Using cyanide sounds like the plot of an old murder mystery
Or copy by someone with no imagination. Yes. One of the after-midnight fillers.
Those old movies always put me to sleep.

BAMBI: But Fairley's permanently asleep.

BLOODHOUND:	Rewind that tape. We need to look at it again. *[he points to the monitor]*
	[the cast quickly reverts to the opening scene]
ASSISTANT:	And here's the host of today's show … welcome to our one and only, the first and final Fairley Fake.
	[enter FF carrying coffee mug]
[Audience goes wild]
[Make-Up Artist rushes in with giant powder puff and dusts everyone]
DIRECTOR:	*[complaining]* Hey, I'm not even on camera.
MAKE-UP ARTIST:	*[dusting self]* Don't panic. It's not flea powder.
FF:	*[snarls at Make-Up Artist in undertone]* Don't worry about them, do me *[beams at camera, drops mug which breaks]* Quick, where's my signature mug? *[Assistant hands her another]*
FF:	*[to Audience]* Welcome, welcome. And how is everyone today?
ASSISTANT:	*[scratching]* Itching to go.
FF:	How can you be more spiritually in tune with your pet-person?
Is the time you spend together quality time?
Do you and your pet-person ever meditate together?
Have you ever spent a day in their shoes? Does your pet-person lead a dog's life?
	[everybody returns to same position on stage as before replay]
BLOODHOUND:	Notice Fairley's coffee mug? After the ad break, it's not the same.

ASSISTANT: That's right. It's mine. She broke hers. Normally we have a supply of FF mugs. We give them to studio audiences. But today we ran out and I wasn't game to tell her. She had to have one. She would have lost is without a mug to hold on camera. But she didn't realise it was mine.

MAKE-UP ARTIST: Fairley put sugar in your coffee mug, earlier on. I remember wondering why? Specially when you're on a diet. And Fairley didn't get drinks for anybody. She treated us all as slaves.

BLOODHOUND: Sugar? Or poison.

ASSISTANT: *[shocked]* Do you reckon she was trying to poison me?

MAKE-UP ARTIST: Why not? She thought you were the one sending her threatening letters.

ASSISTANT: *[indignant]* Why would I want to write to her? It's bad enough putting up with her every day

DIRECTOR: She thought you were after her job. Nothing I could say would convince her otherwise. *[rushes off stage]*

ASSISTANT: She was right. I might say I'd kill for a job like hers, but I'd never kill Fairley. No matter how much everybody hated her.

BLOODHOUND: But maybe her mind was so poisoned against you, she was trying to kill you?

TOM: Maybe she was sending threatening letters to herself and making it appear as if they came from you?

SILVA: *[mysteriously]* Miaow, miaow. Nothing is what it appears.

BLOODHOUND: There seems to be sufficient evidence to suggest that Fairley accidentally killed herself.

BAMBI: What do you mean?

BLOODHOUND: It's possible that Fairley attempted to poison her assistant. By accident she drank from the wrong coffee mug.

ASTRA: Today's stars warned that a mistake in public would be regretted in private. And that storms and heavy weather would last all day. Farewell. May the fur, feather and fins be with you. *[exits]*

DIRECTOR: *[running back on stage excitedly waving sheet of paper]* That's not the only mistake. The front page was left off the ratings. Seems we're rated the number one show, after all.

AUDIENCE: *[explodes in animal noises]*
We knew we were right.
We knew this was the best show. So many animals can't be wrong.
Never under-estimate the public's taste

ASSISTANT: *[dryly]* Or over-estimate it.

DIRECTOR: But now we've lost our original Ms Fake. We've no chat show compere. What can we do now?

ASSISTANT: Can't I be your next Ms Fake?

DIRECTOR: Why not? We could rename you Ms Phoebe Phony. But won't you need an assistant of your own?

SILVA: Miaow, miaow. I'll be Phoebe Phony's assistant. And you can also use me as a New Age Channel.

The Fairly Fake TV Show

	[everybody groups together to clap hands and sing]
ENTIRE CAST:	*[Audience makes appropriate animal noises]* All join paws for the Phoebe show, The Phoebe show, The Phony show. All join paws for the Phony show. And you'll never have a problem again.
AD PERSON:	We apologise for the interference to this program. Our schedule will be resumed as soon as possible.

Relevant issues for discussion

Some relevant topics for discussion include:

- **Public vs private:** For some there's a difference between the public and the private person. Or a difference between acting a role and the real person's beliefs? What would be the problems about 'faking' it in public? Would you need a good memory? An attentive assistant? No feeling of guilt? No conscience?
- **Fake news:** This is a term used for lies. Why might an audience believe faked information? Why and when might a public figure tell lies? What's the difference between lies and diplomacy? How can those who do not tell the truth, be held accountable? Which occupations do audiences tend to believe are the most trustworthy? The least trustworthy? To what extent is it unfair to label an occupation as 'the greatest liars'?
- **Dilemmas:** If the options are to tell the truth, keep quiet or tell a lie, what would you do? To what extent does it depend upon why you are doing it? To protect someone? To save yourself? Not to have to pay? Stand up for your beliefs?
- **Fact vs fiction:** What's the difference between fact and fiction? What's the difference between and opinion and an informed judgement? Subjective and objective opinion?

Activities

1. Judgement

Insects are rarely included as characters in a script.

Create an exchange in a courtroom, between these characters:

- Ant
- Bee
- Beetle
- Cockroach

They are witnesses in a case about infection spreading.

The Judge is a human.

Those in the courtroom can form a chorus.

Create a twist for the end.

2. TV game shows

Create a TV game show in which:

- The contestants are in two teams
- All are plants or insects
- No humans

3. The world of current affairs

You are a current affairs news reporter. There is a most unusual event which has occurred today in a rural area. Animals are involved. You have a 1-minute time slot in which to report. Prepare your script to read on air.

The Mt Paperwork Whodunnit

A satirical 'Whodunnit' for the classroom

A playscript of approximately 40 minutes performance time

Rationale

The conventions of a 'whodunnit' are familiar to most audiences. Whereas, in a satire, a serious subject may be trivialised or inverted, or a trivial subject ridiculed through exaggeration. The aim is to make the audience think differently about a familiar or everyday experience. And maybe suggest a solution. Some TV chat shows give intimate topics the status of an international issue. Thus, they lend themselves to being satirised.

Outline

In this satirical classroom mystery, three contestants arrive at the remote Mt Paperwork retreat near an Old Mine with toxic waste to present their competing visions for the site's future. The Global Entertainments Rep wants to build 'The Big M Theme Park', ambitious pollie Polly MP plans to resettle refugees, and environmental activist Jade dreams of creating a wildlife sanctuary for the mythical SETI creature. But when the Global Entertainment Rep cops it in the heritage-listed Mine Green Store's freezer, everyone becomes both suspect and sleuth in this clever exploration of eco-politics, corporate interests and community values. Students take on character roles and must piece together motives, opportunities and methods to crack the case, all while tackling the big issues of environmental responsibility, heritage preservation and commercial development.

Cast

Allocate roles from the list of Allocated Suspects. Several parts can be played by any gender.

Extra roles can be created, or players can double-up on a character.

The Narrator reads the links and players improvise around their assumed roles.

Props

- 4 courses or snacks in between
- Booklet/running sheet with list of roles
- Pens for 'suspect' notes
- 'Role' name tags
- Lucky dip bag of clues
- An (imaginative) Mt Paperwork trophy for the best solution by a sleuth
- Screen or map of location of body/victim (optional)

Sound effects (SFX)

One person is responsible for sound effects:

- Mobile ringing
- Symbolic music e.g. The Blues, jazz, etc.

Setting

- TV studio with an isolation booth to one side.

> # Invitation
>
> You're invited to help solve a mystery at the Mt Paperwork residential retreat near the Mine in a remote location.
>
> Just for this session, you become both a suspect and maybe a sleuth. One of you will be a victim.
>
> You have been given the role of: ....
>
> Decide on an appropriate name for your character.
>
> Later your character's:
>
> - Motive
> - Opportunity
> - Method
>
> will have to be invented (but you'll have help).

Scenario

Three short-listed contestants are invited to Mt Paperwork retreat in a remote location near an Old Mine with toxic waste. They are to do a feasibility study with the residents on attracting business to the area, using the Old Mine as an Eco-Tourist Attraction.

Time and energy-management are 'hot' eco-political issues, especially as the Old Mine contains leaking toxic waste which may pollute local rivers and crops.

The Rep from Global Entertainments is checking the feasibility of an eco-theme park. Their company could excavate the toxic material from the Old

Mine. They could re-locate the heritage-listed buildings to be set up in a tourist designated site called The Big M Theme Park. Current miners will be given life-time family entry passes to all Theme parks internationally. Work experience is promised for any of their kids.

In return, Global Entertainments want inter-galactic rights to The Big M Theme Park concept. They will pay a .0001 royalty on every entry ticket sold to the theme park (plus GST). This royalty will fund future human impact science ... well a tiny percentage of it.

The Australian politician Polly MP wants to re-settle refugees near the Old Mine. Media-savvy Polly aims to run for PM, so she suggests election slogans on Met weather balloons released from Mt Paperwork range to be shown by satellite on evening television news, ensuring daily coverage at peak times.

Jade, a 'Greenie', wants to save the wildlife at all cost and especially the mythical SETI sighted by Mt Paperwork trail walkers after a 'boys behaving badly weekend', sheltering near the Old Mine. Her solution is to turn the toxic mine into a wildlife sanctuary with artist in residence who recycle toxic waste into safe troglodyte sculptures in the caves.

Facts you need to know

An unusual SETI mythical creature and Southern Hemisphere equivalent of the YETI) has been sighted/photographed near the Old Mine. This is being featured in National Geographic's February issue by a freelance photographer known to some locals.

Big M, a descendant of the original entrepreneurial Mine-owner objects to his ancestor's name being used in any merchandising deals.

On the Old Mine site are several heritage listed buildings such as the Green Store for frozen food supplies and the Red Shed for accommodation of single miners.

Local Small Business Committee is keen on selling naming rights for local features, E.g. Mt Macca's, The Donut's Hole, etc.

The Save-Old-Buildings' (SOB) Heritage Committee doesn't want anything moved from the original mine site, for historic reasons.

The volume of waste in the mine shafts would require considerable expenditure. Global Entertainments' budget is in the billions.

The Global Entertainments Rep is found dead in the freezer in the heritage-listed Mine Green Store alongside the frozen seafood and just below the shelf of frozen peas.

Whodunnit?

How was it done? Why was it done?

In some way, at least one of the following CLUES (supplied in lucky dip bag after the first course) will be involved:

- BERG: an iceberg, a suspect called Berg or a hamburger.
- RING: there was a crucial phone call, an engagement ring or a ring of conspirators.
- KEY: a legend on the map, an ignition key or a mix up of key information.
- NET: an internet site, a net covering evidence or a fishing net.
- BALL: a golf ball, Christmas rum truffle balls, or a special Midwinter Ball.
- GREEN: meaning jealous/envious naïve or with an interest in the environment.
- FORK: fork-lift, fork in the road or a forked tongue telling a lie.

(others can be added)

Allocated Suspects

Weekend guests at Mt Paperwork Retreat are residents or workers near a toxic mine site or are 'experts' brought in to revitalise business in the remote area.

Narrator reads the links and introduces the complications before each course.

- MINE CEO: An urbane diplomat with good knowledge of international law. Their youngest son is involved romantically with Jade. A death-on-site during this administration looks bad on a CV. Would prefer to keep things quiet.
- DEPUTY: Has a screen-saver of Polly on his latest device and has donated to her campaign fund. A political 'groupie' who'd like to be on TV news.
- CHAIR: Previous career as a medical doctor but had a midlife crisis.
- TREASURER: Concerned about the toxic implications. Identical twin brother works for Global Entertainments as a graphic artist and married Treasurer's ex-girlfriend a few months ago.
- CHEF: Agatha Christie fan and knows about poisons, herbs and 57 different spices. Has sculptured an ice Global Entertainments model as a dinner centrepiece. Sacked from former hotel and now works on seasonal contract.
- SECRETARY: Has painted himself into a corner over the SETI issue. His girlfriend is the National Geographic photographer who is claiming an exclusive to get a front cover scoop.
- MINE MECHANIC/ENGINEER: Recently repaired the freezer. Hates frozen peas. Has railway experience on his CV.
- COMMUNICATIONS/COMPUTER NERD: Apparent creator of an interactive mountaineering computer game with million-dollar international potential. Wants media attention. Interested in Global Entertainments sponsorship.
- CHIEF SCIENTIST: Would like Nobel Prize nomination for 'anything'. Loves fishing.
- MET GUY: An Internet gambler with debts. Tired of releasing boring weather balloons and taking readings and has secretly started adding messages to them.
- HELICOPTER (CHOPPER) PILOT: interested in an airfield being developed as it will increase possible contract work.

- CON THE CONSULTANT: Tactless. Loves wildlife and would like the SETI not to be a hoax. Has a time-share in an unusual but relevant location.
- THE REP FROM GLOBAL ENTERTAINMENTS MR/S G. OOFEY: Vegetarian who doesn't eat fish.
- SECURITY CONSULTANT: with links to international undercover agencies and concerns about bio terrorism trialling in remote regions. Pea-like pellets have been discovered.
- POLLY MP: a political candidate aiming for Prime Minister.
- BIG M, the Descendant of the Entrepreneurial Mine-Owner suffers from feelings of inadequacy: scared of heights, is claustrophobic and gets cold feet anywhere dangerous. (The Mine is also known as The Big M)
- FIELD ASSISTANT: Quiz champion and a keen memory for details like exact time-zones but is dubious about SETI and wants to expose the hoax.
- ECO-TOURIST-GUIDE: with camera.
- JADE THE 'GREENIE'. Romantically involved with CEO's offspring.

(Other roles can be added or two can play one role. Each participant stays in role for the entire play period)

Sequence

[7 p.m. The First Course]

NARRATOR: Welcome to the Welcome Dinner. Our chef has done a magnificent job, as usual. We welcome the new faces who have just arrived especially the 'experts' who've come to solve problems the locals feel are unsolvable.

As you all know, the situation of the Old Mine has become increasingly urgent. Toxic waste has been leaking and affecting wildlife. It's a massive clean-up job and beyond our resources. That's why there was an international appeal for a solution and three short-listed people are visiting to check the feasibility of their proposed solutions and ways of attracting business to this area.

Let me introduce, from Global Entertainments, Mr G. Oofey. Oh, not here. I'll tell you about him instead.

His name is G. Oofey. He's here to check on the feasibility of developing a Theme Park. They are proposing to set up an exchange. Their Entertainments section will pay to excavate the toxic material and also set up the heritage listed buildings in a new location as a tourist designated site called The Big M Theme Park. In return Global Entertainments will have inter-galactic rights to The Big M Theme Park and pay a .0001 royalty on every entry ticket sold to the theme park (plus GST of course.)

Now the second short-listed person is the Australian politician Polly MP who wants to re settle refugees in the Mine in return for their

	caretaking as nominal Australians. They will receive bridging sub-passports. Is that correct?
POLLY MP:	Yes, refugees are a global problem and so is pollution. One definition of creativity is to put together two unlikely subjects and come up with an original solution. That's what I'm proposing as timely, especially as there is an election pending.
NARRATOR:	Our third short-listed person is Jade, a 'greenie' who is particularly interested in the SETI seen by some of the guys on their 'boys behaving badly' weekend.
JADE:	Yes, I want to save the wildlife at all cost and especially the SETI which has been sighted by winterers, sheltering near the Mine. My solution is to turn the toxic base into a wildlife sanctuary with resident chemo-eco artists who recycle toxic waste into troglodyte sculptures.
NARRATOR:	Now let's introduce you to everyone else.
	[The Narrator introduces each of the roles, allowing each person to say a little about themselves and why they are on Mt. Paperwork just now.]
NARRATOR:	Now we move onto The Big M.
	As you all know The Big M, around here is known as Sod's Lore. That's the law which states that if anything is to go wrong, or a Big Mistake is to be made, it will go wrong now, here, and in a bigger way than anywhere else.
	So the first thing which goes wrong is…
SFX:	*[SFX-ring ring ring]*

COMMUNICATIONS:	A call for the CEO. The Global Entertainments Rep has been found in an unusual position in the Green Store.
NARRATOR:	Where?
COMMUNICATIONS:	Under the frozen peas and near the frozen seafood … DEAD.
CHAIR:	I'll come with you.

[Chair and CEO leave to investigate]

NARRATOR:	Play the 'cool' background music while we eat our first course, and the CHAIR and CEO get on with their work.
SFX:	*[SFX-symbolic music, e.g. The Blues, jazz, etc.]*

[Chair and CEO return]

CHAIR:	Yes. The Global Entertainments Rep is dead.
NARRATOR:	Condolences. Was it an accident?
CEO:	Unlikely. Everything has been taken care of … Remember the Chair used to be a doctor.
CHAIR:	Probably happened at 6 pm tonight.
NARRATOR:	The dinner started at 7 pm. After we eat our next course, we must examine the motive, opportunity and method of each of you.
TREASURER:	I have a bag of clues here. Maybe each of you should take one and include it in your version of the story.

[All lucky dip for a clue each and have to include that in their own story.
- *BERG: an iceberg, a suspect called Berg or a hamburger.*

- *RING: there was a crucial phone call, an engagement ring or a ring of conspirators.*
- *KEY: a legend on the map, an ignition key or a mix up of key information.*
- *NET: an Internet site, a net covering evidence or a fishing net.*
- *BALL: a golf ball, Christmas rum truffle balls, or a special Midwinter Ball.*
- *GREEN: meaning jealous/envious, naïve or with an interest in the environment.*
- *FORK : fork-lift, fork in the road or a forked tongue telling a lie.]*

NARRATOR: Maybe you could think while eating your next course about the way in which your character was linked with one of these clues?

[Eat second course]

NARRATOR: Now you've had some food for thought, perhaps we can examine motives, clues, methods and opportunity.

Motives are usually:

- Greed
- Sex
- Money
- Ambition or desire for fame
- Covering for another or for yourself
- Altruism
- Clearing own name
- Maintaining reputation

Did you have an opportunity to remove Global Entertainments Rep, if so, how did you do it and why?

[allow discussion]

NARRATOR:	I have two pieces of information to show you. Visuals.
	[introduces the map of the body location and the photo of the SETI]
NARRATOR:	Think about where you fit in this scenario. Or maybe by now, you think someone else did it. Why?
	And we'll have a discussion after the next course. Did you do it, or did someone else? Meanwhile, we'll have some feedback: Dinner!
	[Course 3 served]
NARRATOR:	Time to explain your theories.
	[In character, each need to say where they were at 6pm, what motive they might have had for killing the Rep, the clue they drew, and the method used. They can incriminate themselves or others. Outrageous suggestions are okay if there's some logic]

- Mine CEO
- Deputy
- Chair
- Treasurer
- Chef
- Secretary
- Mine Mechanic/engineer
- Communications/Computer Nerd
- Chief Scientist.
- Met Guy
- Helicopter Pilot
- Con the Consultant
- Security Consultant
- Polly MP

- Big M, the Descendant of the Entrepreneurial Mine-Owner
- Field Assistant
- Eco-Tourist-Guide
- Jade the 'greenie'

* Global Entertainments Rep is dead (but can eat courses).

NARRATOR: Now we are all suspects, since no-one else is on Mt Paperwork.

Please consider, who might have removed the Global Entertainments Rep, how and why.

[Give each an opportunity to present their theories. Either pick the best one, which they can vote for, or have one prepared]

Possibilities:
- Accident which looks like murder
- Collusion of all or of several
- Narrator
- Chair and CEO
- Suicide?

NARRATOR: Thank you for your 'suspect' skills tonight. Just thought you'd like to know what happened afterwards.

Global Entertainments decides to re-site The Big M theme park to Darwin/Alice Springs/Northern Territory because the new Melbourne-Darwin railway will bring more tourists to the area, and in a hot climate people will be especially attracted to an underground 'cool' park.

Polly MP becomes PM, after she puts A for Antarctica in front of her name (by deed poll) and gets all the donkey votes, or due to climate changes all the Met balloons carrying her name float across Australia.

Jade creates a Wall of Fame for all the Firsts in the Environment. The First one to climb Mt Paperwork. The first sleuth to solve a mystery with a believable solution ....

[Eat course 4]

NARRATOR: I'd now like to give out the special award for the best solution by a sleuth tonight.

The award goes to .... because ......

Relevant issues for discussion

Some relevant topics for discussion include:

- **Consider character motivations:** Who had the most to gain from hiding the toxic waste dumping? Examine how money, power and reputation influenced different characters' choices and actions throughout the play.
- **Responsibility:** Environmental crimes often involve complex webs of responsibility. Discuss who bears the real responsibility - the business leaders who made the decisions, the politicians who may have turned a blind eye, or the workers who actually dumped the waste? Consider how accountability changes at different levels of power.
- **Evidence in environmental crimes:** In solving environmental crimes, evidence can be hidden or destroyed. Consider what makes investigating environmental crimes particularly challenging.

Activities

1. 'Whodunnit?'

Whodunnit is a term often used to describe mysteries. These are the questions a mystery writer has to answer in the story to be fair to the readers.

Which is your favourite mystery you have read or seen on screen? Can you answer motive, opportunity and method for this story?

What is a 'red herring?'

Myster and crime motives are usually:

- Greed
- Sex
- Money
- Ambition/desire for fame
- Covering for another or for self

- Altruism: doing something for no personal gain
- Clearing own name
- Maintaining reputation

Can you think of any other motive? Like an accident? A mistake?

2. Satire

A satire often 'sends up' and pokes fun by exaggerating silly habits. The aim may be to embarrass, to stop the habit or to laugh together.

There's a difference between laughing AT to make the victim seem foolish and laughing WITH because we all do things like that at times.

What silly/useless rule applies around your place that you would like to change?

3. Forensics

Are you good with details? If you're interested in solving problems, a career in forensics may suit. This includes technicians and professionals in medicine, science, finance and legal areas and ranges from solving serious crimes to working on legal cases in the courts.

Countries differ in the names and jobs. A forensic pathologist may be called a medical examiner in some areas and be qualified in medicine and law.

Find the names of three jobs which require forensic skills – e.g. Forensic accountants are experts in financial crime and work to uncover fraud and protect bank accounts against fraudulent activity. They examine financial records and accounts that may be used as evidence.

What does the word 'forensic' mean?

4. Facts and fantasy

Often there is a difference between the speed at which things happen in a mystery shown on screen, and in real life. But the writer needs to research to make sure it is possible scientifically. Attention to detail is needed.

In earlier times, the forensic science available now, like DNA matching hadn't been heard of.

Poison was the most common method for mystery writers like Agatha Christie, as she had worked in a pharmacy. Females often used poison because it was available from plants in the home garden, pesticides or rat poison in the garden shed. It could often be slipped into food by whoever was cooking. Not all mysteries are homicides where someone dies.

You are the director-producer of a mystery movie which is a re-make of an earlier, famous film. The new version is set in present day. What might you need to change? Clues? Use of technology? Location? Occupations? Motives?

5. Sleuths

Your 'sleuth' needs to have expert knowledge and be able to move around easily. That's why many were newspaper reporters or investigative journalists in earlier stories.

Police procedurals used police detectives. Currently, pathologists are popular as fictional sleuths. Your sleuth also needs a reason for solving the mystery? Money? Fame? Clearing the name of self or a friend?

As mysteries have become more skilled, the sleuth needs to have more skills too. Or have someone as a friend or 'off-sider' who knows 'stuff'.

Create your own sleuth:

- Name
- Age
- Skills/Job
- Background
- Appearance: height, favourite clothes, gadgets, etc.
- Reason for solving the mystery

Create a Sleuths' Gallery on a classroom wall or digitally.

The Minutes of Time

A readers theatre script for secondary students

A playscript of approximately 40 minutes performance time

Rationale

Readers' Theatre is when actors sit in a semi-circle reading in turn, using an appropriate hat or prop. Alternatively, it can be performed at an appropriate site such as a museum or clocktower or on stage with the actors 'dressing up'.

Outline

'The Minutes of Time' is a playful and thought-provoking Readers' Theatre piece set in the year 3000 on Planet Itus, where time rather than money is the currency of choice. Through a Virtual Museum that allows time travel, characters explore past and future ways of organising society and conducting meetings, offering both satire of current committee structures and insights into how future societies might value and measure success.

Cast

Several parts can be played by any gender. The chorus size is flexible and some can take extra parts for a larger or smaller cast size.

NARRATOR: has old style watch with a second hand.

A CHORUS (any number): who want to SAVE time (the eco group who wish to preserve).

B CHORUS (any number): who want to SPEND time (pro-tourist attractions where time can be spent).

C CHORUS (any number): who KEEP time (song and dance act) with musical instruments to keep the beat. e.g. drum.

WATCH-DOG: with large timepiece around neck.

TIMEKEEPER: with stopwatch.

PART-TIME PERSON eager to please and asks questions.

FULL-TIMER: a little pompous.

POLITICAL PIRATE: who operates on self-interest.

GUIDE TO THE PAST

FUTURES GUIDE

OLDEN DAYS COMMITTEE:

- Chairman
- Treasurer
- Assistant Treasurer (who can juggle balls)
- Secretary
- Union Delegate Fussy
- Program Co-Ordinator
- Community Rep.
- Lex, the Legal person
- Finn, the Finance person

Props

- Hat, clocks and watches
- Drums to keep the beat
- Balls for juggling
- Agenda
- Bundle of papers for committee reports
- Photo of a committee

Sound effects (SFX)

One person is responsible for sound effects:

- Dance music
- Alarms

Setting

Planet Itus in the Year of 3000 when units of time, not dollars are the currency. A Virtual Museum allows travel to the past and the future. The Minutes of Time meeting is being held.

Script

NARRATOR: Have you ever lost time? Where did it go?
If your watch stops, does time stop?
If the Internet is down, how do you tell the time?
On the Planet Itus, in the year 3000, TIME is the currency.
They don't use dollars.
They use minutes.
So, time is valued. Even second-hand time.
[looks at watch with second hand]
That's why we're at the Virtual Museum today.

UNION DELEGATE: We agreed that each time the Minutes of Time group would meet in a different site. Today it is the Virtual Museum. We're going to do some free time travel. Union discounts. My members have agreed. I can speak for them. And I can travel on their behalf.

A CHORUS: We want to SAVE time.

B CHORUS: We want to spend time and get a good return. We like to visit scenic tourist spots during visiting hours, and we like tourists to spend time with us too.

C CHORUS: *[moving to the beat]*
We keep time, very well.

WATCH-DOG: It's time to start the meeting. Is everyone here?

PART-TIME PERSON: I'm a part-time person, but I am here.

WATCH-DOG: What do you do the rest of the time?

PART-TIME PERSON: It depends where I am at the time. Past. Present. Or future. I'm flexible. Sometimes my

	body is present, and my mind is somewhere else.
FULL-TIMER:	I'm a full-time member.
WATCH DOG:	Are you prepared to invest minutes, hours or even weeks in this project?
FULL-TIMER:	Yes.
PART-TIME PERSON:	If I'm only involved part-time does that mean I'm not worth as much? Aren't my ideas valued in the same way?
FINN:	Values are affected by the International Exchange. I'm Finn, the Finance Person and I'm the expert on value.
	Crossing the International Date Line can mean 'gaining' or 'losing' a day. What if that missing day were your birthday, or a particularly difficult one you did not wish to repeat?
	That would be a great loss.
LEX:	… or a great gain. It's all a matter of interpretation. Legal interpretations are worked out …
WATCH DOG:	… at chargeable minutes.
LEX:	Of course. People accept you at YOUR valuation. And I consider that my time is valuable. Lex is my name. Law is my game. I'm the Legal Person in this group.
SFX:	*[SFX-drums]*
NARRATOR:	Time to drum up a little interest.
C CHORUS:	*[do a song-and-dance act]* We're the Chorus

The Minutes of Time

| | The Bottom Line.
| | Our figures are great
| | And this time we're fine.
| | We keep time.
| | We keep time.

DELEGATE: *[officiously]* You'll be fined if you interrupt again. I'm the official Delegate. This is the Timetable on which we have agreed. No going outside this.

B CHORUS: We want people to spend some time in our area.
See our eco-tourist attractions.
Like the Virtual Museum.
So, we can learn about how they did our jobs in the olden days.

TIME-KEEPER: I'm the Time-Keeper. In the olden days, they used to call me a Banker. They used to have buildings where money was kept. Tellers were the bank workers who gave out the money. People made deposits or withdrew amounts of money.

Banks offered interest to people.

A CHORUS: We're the A Chorus.
We want to save time, and other things.
That's why we have recycled the past in this Virtual Museum.
You can key in the year or the ritual you wish to visit.
C is the special today. C for Committees.
These were popular rituals in the early part of the twenty-first century.

GUIDE: I'm the Guide to the Past.

	I work for the Virtual Museum and will guide you through Committees.
	Many virtual rooms of these.
ALL:	*[call out]* Board Rooms.
	Boring Rooms.
	Sitting Rooms.
	Lounge Rooms.
	Waiting Rooms!
GUIDE TO THE PAST:	In the olden days, the meetings were called Committees.
	Here is a scan of a committee.
	This is an example of an Agenda.
	This is a sub-committee.
NARRATOR:	See, the Virtual Museum can offer you these insights to the Past ways ... And we have some holograms of committee members.
	Virtually all of them.
GUIDE TO THE PAST:	Here is the Chairman.
CHAIR:	*[Bows]* I'm a virtual Chair. An old Chair. Practically an antique. I sit on the Board.
GUIDE TO THE PAST:	A committee was what we call a Time-Bank these days. People used to invest their time in meeting together, in a certain room, at regular intervals.
FULL-TIMER:	Why did they do that?
GUIDE TO THE PAST:	Because they thought they'd make a difference.
COMMUNITY REP:	My family complains about the time this committee takes.
TREASURER:	I'm a virtual Treasurer. In the olden days I looked after the money. Or told them where

The Minutes of Time 97

	the money should have been if people had paid their subs on time.
ASSISTANT TREASURER:	
	I'm the Assistant Treasurer. Known as the ASS for short.
GOOD TIME GUY:	*[Interrupting]* Did you fool around? Did you have a good time?
ASSISTANT TREASURER:	
	[Juggling] Juggling was my skill. Needed a sense of balance. Catch? *[throws balls to Treasurer]*
TREASURER:	Some balancing act! Our books had to be balanced.
SECRETARY:	I'm the Secretary. Minutes were my job.
WATCH DOG:	*[Enthusiastically]* Ah! You predicted the future currency?
ASSISTANT SECRETARY:	
	No. Minutes were just the name of the notes.
DELEGATE:	*[Eagerly]* Bank notes?
SFX:	*[SFX-dance music]*
C CHORUS:	*[Dancing]* Musical notes, like this matter more.
GOOD TIME GUY:	I'm a good time guy. I like to play around. I'm just an old-time dancer. I like the olden days and the way things were done then.
NARRATOR:	Who will partner the members from the Past? Choose the one whose role was closest to yours. Try an old-time dance.

[Pair and dance with opposites from committee of the past. Chorus members dance with each other.]

[Lines can be swapped or both can say them]

TREASURER: *[To Time-keeper]* Excuse me Time-Keeper. Money was my currency. Time is yours. We seem to be in the same line of business. Would you like to dance?

[They do/don't keep time well together]

I'm having a really bad time …
I'm having a good time …

REP/PART-TIME PERSON: Time-out is important. Especially if the other person has big feet!

PROGRAM COORDINATOR/FULLTIMER: It's said that if you can dance together, you will get along in life.

SECRETARY: I'm the Secretary. I did keep the Minutes, so I guess we have something in common.

DELEGATE: Time off is more important. Our staff deserve it.

ASS TREASURER/POLITICAL PIRATE: Will you lead or follow? Sorry. I don't dance to anyone else's tune.

SFX: *[SFX-alarm rings]*

ALL: A time-bomb!

CHAIR: *[Looks at watch]* This is all second-hand time. I mean time you recycle, like money you re-invested in the past.

ALL:	TIME OUT! We must withdraw from the past. Deposit us in Year 3000.
CHAIR:	For the time being, we will say goodbye. Hope you have learnt from visiting our committee.
PART-TIMER:	What will happen in the future? The past used to count the money. We check the time in the future what will they do?
POLITICAL PIRATE:	Another currency. One in which I have shares.
FUTURES GUIDE:	As the Futures Guide, I can offer more than one possible future. The Guide to the Past can give you only one story. I have many available.
GUIDE TO THE PAST:	We need to learn from our mistakes in the past.
FUTURES GUIDE:	But we're moving into the future now. It's a different scenario. No longer can value be measured by time or moneys. The new currency is ... Satisfaction
WATCH-DOG:	*[Sighing resignedly]* I'll have to retrain, again.
TIME-KEEPER:	I don't understand these words.
FULL-TIMER:	Happiness? Satisfaction? How would you measure units of that?
FINN:	Can't tax that!
LEX:	Legally hard to quantify bliss.
POLITICAL PIRATE:	Satisfaction. Whether a project worked out. Whether it was finished. Whether people enjoyed working together.
NARRATOR:	This is the year 3000 on the Planet Itus.

All have returned safely from the past. The next excursion from the Virtual Museum will be into the Future. We will explore future options.
Be here for the next Minutes of Time meeting when we will invest time in a future project.

POLITICAL PIRATE: I have shares in that.

LEX: Isn't that a conflict of interest. Shouldn't you declare it?

POLITICAL PIRATE: That's no conflict of interest for me.
Whatever the currency, self-interest is always my law of survival.

Relevant issues for discussion

Some relevant topics for discussion include:

- **Time as currency:** How does putting a numerical value on every minute change its meaning? Consider how our society already measures time through wages, billable hours and 'free time'. Question whether precise measurement of time makes us value it more or diminishes its true worth.

- **Organisational structures and human behaviour:** Examine the play's satirical characters (Union Delegate, Political Pirate, Part-Timer) and what they reveal about how organisations function. Consider whether modern meetings and committees mirror these futuristic portrayals. Question if our current organisational systems are truly logical or effective.

- **Future perspectives on present practices:** Through the Virtual Museum setting, explore how future societies might interpret and misunderstand our current practices. Consider which aspects of our present-day society might seem incomprehensible to people in 3000, and which of our common practices they might completely misinterpret.

- **Measuring the unmeasurable:** Analyse the progression from money to time to satisfaction as currency. Question our society's need to quantify everything and consider what aspects of life (like Lex's 'bliss') resist measurement. Explore whether some things lose their inherent value when we try to measure them.

- **Adaptation versus constancy:** Compare characters' different responses to change: the Watch-Dog's constant retraining versus the Political Pirate's unchanging self-interest. Consider what aspects of society and human nature truly change over time, and what remains constant despite technological and social evolution.

Activities

1. Currency reimagined

Working in small groups of 3-4 students, participants design their own society with a unique form of currency (such as knowledge, creativity, kindness or dreams) and develop a complete system showing how their currency would be measured, earnt and spent, along with analysing potential benefits and problems of their system. Each group presents their currency concept to the class, followed by a discussion exploring how different currency systems might affect social equality, what our current money-based system says about our values, and how alternative currencies could address current social problems.

2. Readers' theatre workshop

Students explore different performance styles by dividing into three groups, each taking a different approach to the same scene: traditional Readers' Theatre (sitting, minimal movement), enhanced Readers' Theatre (standing, with props and basic movement), and full performance (movement, character interaction). After each group performs the same three-minute section of the script, the class analyses how different presentation styles affected the message, which elements were most effective, how vocal techniques changed between styles, and how the audience experience differed, culminating in creating a 'Best Practices' guide for Readers' Theatre.

3. Time capsule project

Students create their own 'Virtual Museum' exhibit about life in their current time period by selecting 5-7 items that represent important aspects of current society, writing museum-style descriptions and future-perspective analyses for each item, and creating either a virtual or physical display that includes descriptions, analysis and interactive elements. Students present their exhibits to the class whilst their peers role-play as visitors from the year 3000, encouraging them to think deeply about how future generations might interpret our current way of life and values.

www.ingramcontent.com/pod-product-compliance
Lightning Source LLC
Chambersburg PA
CBHW050301120526
44590CB00016B/2440